Dear Amy,

You have made

to do political theory and to

well. Thank you for making

it a pleasure to work on

this project!

Best wishes,

Amy

PUNISHMENT, PROPERTY AND JUSTICE

Dedication

To my students at the United Nations International School and the New Jersey Governor's School of Public Issues.

Punishment, Property and Justice

Philosophical foundations of the death penalty and welfare controversies

COREY LANG BRETTSCHNEIDER
Princeton University, USA

Ashgate

DARTMOUTH

Aldershot • Burlington USA • Singapore • Sydney

Published by
Ashgate Publishing Ltd
Gower House
Croft Road
Aldershot
Hants GU11 3HR
England

Ashgate Publishing Company
131 Main Street
Burlington, VT 05401-5600 USA

Ashgate website: http://www.ashgate.com

British Library Cataloguing in Publication Data

Brettschneider, Corey Lang
   Punishment, property and justice : philosophical foundations of the
   death penalty and welfare controversies. – (Law,
   justice and power)
   1. Justice (Philosophy) 2. Capital punishment – Moral and
   ethical aspects 3. Public welfare – Moral and ethical
   aspects
   I. Title
   172.2

Library of Congress Cataloging-in-Publication Data

Brettschneider, Corey Lang
   Punishment, property and justice: philosophical foundations of the death penalty and
   welfare controversies / Corey Lang Brettschneider.
       p. cm.
   Includes bibliographical references.
   ISBN 0-7546-2064-6 (HB)
       1. Justice. 2. Punishment. 3. Capital punishment. 4. Distributive justice. 5. Public
   welfare. I. Title.

JC578 .B685 2000
172'.2—dc21   00-44806

ISBN 0 7546 2064 6
Printed and bound by Athenaeum Press, Ltd.,
Gateshead, Tyne & Wear.

Contents

Acknowledgements   vii

Introduction: Why Justice is Relevant to Politics   1

Part I   The Death Penalty and Punishment

1   Introduction to Part I: The Death Penalty and Punishment   13
2   Revenge, Pity and Empathy: Common Roots of the Death
     Penalty Debate   15
3   Emotion Defended   21
4   General Deterrence   23
5   Singular Deterrence and Rehabilitation   27
6   Retribution   33
7   Nietzsche's Critique: The Link Between Deterrence, Retribution
     and Revenge   43
8   From Punishment to Ethics and Political Justice   47
9   Philosophical Foundations: Utilitarianism and Deterrence   51
10   Hybrid Theory: Rawls's Act Utilitarianism   57
11   Philosophical Foundations: Retributivism and Kantian
     Deontology   59
12   *Furman* vs. *Georgia*   65
13   The Link Between Retributive and Distributive Justice   73

Part II   Welfare, Property and Distributive Justice

14   Introduction to Part II: Is There a Right to Welfare?   77
15   Locke on Property, Distributive Justice and Welfare   83
16   Rousseau and the Fundamental Right to Welfare   97
17   Rawls's Theory of Justice   111
18   Walzer and the Critique of Primary Goods   125
19   Rawls, Work and the Free-rider Problem   129
20   Nozick, Desert and Natural Talent   133

21 Should There be a Constitutional Right to Welfare?   135
22 Marx and the Radical Critique of the Right to Welfare   139
23 Distributive Justice, Property and the Right to Welfare   143

Conclusion   147

Bibliography   149
Index   151

Acknowledgements

This book is the product of years of conversations with teachers, students, colleagues and friends. My thanks are due first to Paul Hurley who introduced me to philosophy of law when I was a student in his class at Pomona College. Themes from our discussions (and disagreements) are present throughout this entire book. Part I is in many ways the result of a class we designed together and co-taught, entitled "The Criminal Justice System and Its Justifications," for the Pomona College Summer Seminar Institute of 1995. I would also like to thank Lee McDonald, John Seery and Steve Erickson, all of whom worked with me at Pomona on issues related to this book.

The bulk of this book was written at Princeton University, and I could not have completed it without the help and encouragement of three people. First, Amy Gutmann generously gave me detailed comments and suggestions on the entire manuscript. Part II on welfare and distributive justice in particular is largely the outgrowth of a series of exchanges between us. She has been a tremendous help and is a role model scholar. Second, I have benefited enormously from continued exchanges on welfare and the death penalty with George Kateb. The section on Locke and welfare evolved from a series of discussions we had in the autumn of 1999. His passion and pure intellectual honesty make me wish I could do a better job of answering his criticisms. Third, Mariah Zeisberg provided detailed comments about the substance, style and structure of Part II. Mariah has been all one could hope for in a colleague and a friend. In addition to these three scholars, Peter Singer gave me much to think about in regard to utilitarianism in general and as it applies to punishment. I only wish I had more space here to deal with his views more directly.

Throughout this project, I have been lucky enough to be both tolerated and encouraged by my good friends and family. Allison Weisz has been my main companion in all aspects of personal and intellectual life and has given me consistent support throughout this project. In particular, I would like to thank her for her detailed and insightful comments on the entire manuscript. Meyer Lang, Kim Brettschneider, Susan Brettschneider, Eric Brettschneider, Lane Brettschneider, Jeanne Rostaing and Robert Klopfer deserve thanks as well for their support. I would also like to thank John Leibovitz and Jacob Schmutz for suffering through a diatribe on retributivism during a long road trip to Vermont.

At Cambridge University, during work on my M.Phil., I had many conversations related to these topics. In particular I would like to thank Melissa Lane and Gareth Stedman Jones for helping me to develop many of the ideas in this book.

I also owe a tremendous debt to my friends, colleagues and students at the United Nations International School and the Governor's School of Public Issues. It was in teaching at these amazing institutions that I formulated the idea for this book. Colleagues and friends from both schools who deserve special thanks include Hilary Ainger, Peter Atkinson, Jerome Dutilloy, John Eck, David Evans, Tom Siefring, Selmataw Wolle, Adrian Rodriguez and Claude Taylor. In addition, I would like to thank three of my philosophy students from the United Nations International School, Fatin Abbas, Nick Schretzman and Mathew Schneider-Mayerson, for reading and commenting on parts of this manuscript.

Finally, I would like to thank the series editor, Austin Sarat, for coaching me through the book-writing process, and Paul Safier, for suggesting the title.

Introduction: Why Justice is Relevant to Politics

This is a book about justice. In the pages to follow I want to demonstrate that debates about justice in political and legal philosophy are relevant to the political and legal controversies currently being discussed in the editorial pages of major newspapers, in our classrooms and at dinner tables throughout the nation and the world. Specifically, I want to show that the participants in debates over capital punishment and welfare–arguably two of the most pressing and controversial issues we as a society face today–should look to philosophical theories about politics to gain a better appreciation of the assumptions and foundations of their positions. I have divided the book into two parts. Part I is an attempt to connect the death penalty debate with the philosophical controversy over justice and punishment. Part II is an attempt to connect the debate over whether there is a right to welfare with the philosophical debate over distributive justice.

In our time many people are skeptical toward the concept of justice. For many, the term is merely an empty abstraction used to bolster one's position. On a recent CNN round table over the federal budget, one commentator pounded the table and demanded that the other side cave in to the "just demands" of his party. Here and elsewhere the term "justice" served merely as an argumentative device that seemed to do little to move the participants in these discussions beyond the impasse they often reach. If the term merely serves as a rhetorical device in argument, how then is it possible to lift the level of debate on actual political and legal issues through a philosophical examination of "justice"?

If we take Plato's accounts of conversation in ancient Athens literally, there was a time when it was easy to spark a general inquiry into the meaning of justice. According to his dialogues a mere inquiry into justice sparked discussions that lasted several days.[1] Such an impassioned discussion would be hard to start in the contemporary world. This point was brought home to me at a dinner party soon after I accepted a job teaching political philosophy. After hearing that I teach political philosophy for a living, several times people remarked: "One thing I know is that philosophy has nothing to do with politics."

The reactions were hardly better when I began teaching high school political philosophy classes. On my first day, I attempted to begin discussion as if I were Socrates in ancient Athens. I asked simply: "What is justice?" The result was a long silence. Eventually a few students suggested a few dictionary-type definitions: "Justice is getting what you deserve" was a common response; "Justice is treating everyone equally" a few volunteered. After a few attempts the discussion died and someone asked, "Why is this relevant to anything now?"

In contrast, if I began class with a question about a public issue, animated conversation followed. Students responded to the issues we will deal with in this book with well-developed arguments and were eager to engage each other in debate. Should we have a death penalty? Do the poorest in our society have a right to welfare payments from the government? These questions seemed relevant in a way that simply asking about justice was not.

Once these discussions began, it was not hard to make the transition to conversations about justice. Discussions about the death penalty, for instance, usually began with each student taking a position for or against the penalty and then stating several reasons at the same time why their stance was correct. Pro-death penalty students mentioned statistics showing that the penalty deters others from future crime, that it is cheaper than life imprisonment, and that it avenges heinous crime. Anti-death penalty students argued that the penalty was cruel and in the same sentence disputed the factual claims their interlocutors made about deterrence and cost. When I brought it to these students' attention that they had mentioned several different types of reasons for their position, they had no choice but to begin theorizing. Why, they were forced to ask, is punishment justified in the first place?

Those who prioritized criteria such as deterrence or cost, when questioned, usually stated that the consequences of punishment are the most important factors in deciding whether or not a punishment should be given, as well as how much punishment should be given. Similarly, those who emphasized "cruelty" or "getting one's due" often argued that punishment should be given out in regard to the act itself. Discussion of the specific death penalty issue therefore easily becomes a debate over what criterion justifies punishment in the first place. This question, as I will show in the pages to follow, is a question about justice.

A similar pattern took place when students debated the welfare question. They began with positions on whether or not welfare is a right. They were soon, however, led to discussions of what the role of the state is in redistributing wealth. Those who strongly defended a view of welfare as a right found themselves defending views of justice which claim the state's fundamental role is to ensure material subsistence. Those who argued that there is no such right soon found themselves arguing for a libertarian view of the role of the state.

This book is written in the hope of demonstrating the same point that has been revealed to me through teaching: justice is still relevant to our most pressing political issues. I want to connect our contemporary political debates with the discussion philosophers have traditionally had about punishment and the proper distribution of wealth. Once the philosophical conversation about retributive justice is brought to bear on the death penalty debate, I believe all parties will gain a deeper understanding of their positions. Similarly, our current debates about welfare will have greater clarity once they are connected to the philosophical debate over distributive justice.

Objections to Justice

Many thinkers who align themselves with the liberal tradition of political philosophy are engaged in the philosophical project of trying to bring considerations of justice to bear on public issues. It is therefore this tradition that I will largely be concerned with in the pages to follow. There are many contemporary thinkers outside this tradition, however, who would challenge outright my claim that justice is relevant. Before I outline the content of the chapters to follow, it is necessary to say a few words about why these anti-liberal thinkers object to the term "justice" and any attempt of an author to show that it is relevant to contemporary problems.

The Objection from Ideology and Power

The first objection comes from thinkers who place themselves in the Marxist tradition; it can be labelled the "objection from ideology and power." On this view, the concept of justice and arguments regarding its nature merely serve to mask the economic and power relations of a given time period. Marxist thinkers argue that by engaging in a discussion that attempts to locate the meaning of justice we are only serving to reinforce the dominant class's hold over the rest of the population. In contrast to a conversation about justice, an analysis of power relations would reveal the reality that some groups in our society dominate others with no justification. In examining punishment, for example, these thinkers might point out the contrast between the slogans on the outside of our courts and the reality that happens inside those institutions. In New York City, the criminal court has engraved on its outside wall a slogan about how the accused will receive justice inside. The reality, however, is that the poor are given overworked lawyers who are paid little, while the wealthy get better representation. In addition, those who are accused of crimes come overwhelmingly from the poorest strata of society. Marxist theorists would argue that by discussing justice, philosophers are ignoring this oppression. A theoretical framework which dismissed the type of slogans we found outside courtrooms and the very concept of justice, they argue, would bring us much closer to diagnosing the real problems of society.

The objection from ideology cannot be dismissed easily. For one thing, the claim seems to have a good amount of empirical evidence behind it. There have in fact been many instances of brutal oppression which have been accompanied by elaborate theoretical claims cloaked in the language of justice, the same language I want to argue is helpful to use in exploring contemporary issues. For instance, an elaborate and apologetic philosophical literature of justice existed during apartheid in South Africa. In the United States, many of the same founders who invoked the language of justice also argued for slavery.

I do not, however, believe it is necessary to completely abandon the language of justice despite its bloodstained history. As I will demonstrate, justice claims are in fact linked to some arguments that would demand massive change, even revolutionary change, in contemporary society. There is nothing in the notion of justice itself that precludes genuine critique of the type that the Marxist wants. The objection from ideology fails because the language of justice which has been used to support oppression can in fact be used to criticize oppression.[2]

It is true that many of the arguments from justice that I will explore throughout this text are justifications of the status quo. Once the language of justice is accepted, however, it is no longer possible to simply dismiss these claims as mere ideology. Rather, one who wants to argue that a certain conception of justice is unacceptable faces the task of arguing why a given position is unjust. I want to suggest that this obligation to engage in argument renders any arguments which are made in the language of justice superior to those made solely in terms of power. This is true for two reasons. First, a community of argument is formed in which, although people disagree, they are united in the attempt to find whether or not their specific policy formulations live up to a conception of justice. A diagnosis of power, in contrast, posits competing interests, which have no hope of genuine consensus. Call this the dialogical aspect of the language of justice. Second, those who use the language of justice can step outside of the emotional territory that often surrounds debates about the death penalty and welfare, leading to stalemates, into a conversation that is less loaded and more productive. In other words, philosophical arguments that rely on the discourse of justice, I believe, are less likely than those using the discourse of power to provoke knee-jerk answers. Call this the critical distance of justice.

Neither the critical distance nor the dialogical aspect of the language of justice is available to the theorist who thinks solely in terms of power. For them, politics is the project of a scientist, merely observing the way individuals and groups dominate each other. In contrast to the theorist of power, in this text I rely on the notion that political theorists throughout the centuries have talked to each other through a common language. In this language the concept of justice is seen as a desirable end. The dialogical aspect of justice leads to a model of conversation about society's basic institutions in which all arguments are taken seriously. In contrast, the argument from ideology would dismiss the arguments of those in power outright simply as a result of their social position. The critical distance of justice, however, demands that we abstract from our social roles and listen to the arguments of all who make normative claims about the just society.

I should admit that I believe that if the language of justice is taken seriously, one is led to a conception of society that must be very critical of the status quo. My anti-death penalty and pro-welfare views certainly inform the arguments in this book; however, my goal in the pages to follow is not to argue for welfare rights and against captial punishment but rather to demonstrate how the language of justice can help us to better understand these two pressing controversies.

For some thinkers the welfare and death penalty controversies cannot be resolved. They would argue that examining disagreements in terms of justice only leads to more disagreement. Such a person might ask, "Why bother analyzing contemporary issues in terms of justice since both philosophical and political conversations lack answers?" Call this the objection from relativism. I take this objection to be a serious challenge to my entire project. Like the argument from ideology it must also be explored before we begin to examine contemporary controversies through the lens of justice.

The Objection from Moral Relativism

Much of the criticism of the commitment to justice stems from an objection that can broadly be labelled "moral relativism." While post-modernists and other philosophers have certainly developed sophisticated versions of relativism, here I am interested in exploring relativism in its most common form. I take this version of relativism, which, following Bernard Williams, I label "vulgar relativism," to be one of the main objections to my project. It is certainly widely held, especially in the United States, and therefore it is worth exploring.

The relativist will argue that neither arguments about justice nor arguments about contemporary controversies can be resolved because all moral and political statements are true only for the person advancing a political position.

In arguments about the death penalty, for instance, a student will often object that a position, say, for the death penalty is merely an "opinion" that is true only for the person speaking.

What is interesting about the objection is that it almost always takes place after a raging debate in which many positions and arguments have been advanced. Rather than furthering discussion, the objection from relativism often stifles it. In practical political discussion relativism therefore seems oddly misplaced. From a practical point of view, relativism is unhelpful and nonsensical. Of course, the fact that the relativist position is a conversation-stopper for others is not in itself an argument against it. The fact that it contradicts the views of the same people that advance it, however, is a valid argument. It is often the case that the same people who earlier in a conversation were taking a specific position then make the relativist claim. In a conversation about the death penalty, for instance, someone might claim that the death penalty is wrong and then go on to make the relativist claim that there are no right answers in politics. If the claim against the death penalty was correct, however, this would necessitate that the claim in defense of relativism be false. If relativism is true that means that all claims, including one's own, must be relative; therefore, there is little use in making them.

Bernard Williams brings out the self-refuting tendencies of relativists when he examines the argument that industrialized nations should not intervene in the internal conflicts of smaller countries.[3] On this view, often held by anthropologists, it is wrong to intervene in the moral life of another culture. Relativists often use this claim to support their view. How, however, can one make an argument against intervention if no statements can be true? It seems that relativism in effect undercuts the very policy relativists want to advance.

Needless to say, I do not accept the relativist claim. If I did it would be very hard to write a book in the hope of helping to further discussion about political controversies. Discussion, for the relativists, is useless at best. Nonetheless the view is prevalent enough that at points in the book I think it is necessary to examine the impact of the objection from relativism on contemporary controversies. I do this, for instance, in the section on objections to Retributivism. In addition, although I reject the argument from ideology, I also think it is important enough to be examined where relevant. I therefore devote whole sections at two places to the objection. In the discussion of punishment, I devote a section to Nietzsche. In the discussion of welfare and distributive justice, I devote a section to Marx.

The Relationship Between Justice and Equality

I have endeavoured to write a book about the relevance of justice to contemporary issues. It would be impossible for me to do so, however, without focusing a great deal of the discussion on the relationship between equality and justice. The two concepts are greatly interrelated for almost all of the theorists we will examine in the following pages. Despite the close link, however, the concepts of equality we will examine are tools used to elaborate on concepts of justice and/or are derived from concepts of justice. Theorists often start with the assumption that justice in society is worth pursuing. It is less obvious to them that equality is equally desirable. Instead, for many theorists equality plays a role in helping either to formulate principles of justice or is an aspect of the just society.

In Part I, on the death penalty and punishment, equality is relevant but plays a secondary role to justice. The unequal application of the death penalty toward African-American defendants in the United States is itself a major argument against using the penalty. While this argument has a great deal of validity in evaluating the penalty's use in the United States, it does not necessarily rule out the possibility that the death penalty could be just in a more ideal world. Without ignoring the impact that the unequal application of the penalty has had, I focus on the question of whether the penalty would be just in a world without discrimination.

In Part II, both welfarist and anti-welfarist theorists also prioritize justice over equality. Rawls and Rousseau both offer a theory of justice which is based on the notion that each citizen has equal value. In formulating principles of justice this premise must always be respected. In addition to arguing that equality is necessary in developing principles of justice, both theorists also claim that justice necessitates egalitarian distributions of wealth. Egalitarian distributions are not, however, equal distributions. The theories of justice offered by Nozick and Locke, by contrast offer a view in which equality plays less of a role both in the development of conceptions of justice and in the distributions that result from such conceptions. For instance, in Locke's view, the natural law, rather than equal citizenship, form the basis of the state. While the law applies equally to all, it does not rest on the very notion of equality. In addition, it necessitates neither an equal nor egalitarian distribution of wealth.

The Challenge to Philosophical Foundations

So far I have said a few words about justice, equality and objections to the concept of justice. Before outlining the rest of the book that will follow this introduction, it is necessary to say something about the other major phrase in my title: philosophical foundations. Throughout the history of political thought, writers have attempted to argue for various versions of the just state by appealing to ideas of legitimacy. For Plato, the state would only be just when it rested on the foundation of the ultimate truth in the world, the form of the good. This truth, like some later notions of God, could not be fully described in words. It was a foundation that could only be alluded to through metaphor. For Plato, the foundation of the state, the form of the good, was best understood as the source of all knowledge and truth, much as the sun is the source of all human light. For later Enlightenment thinkers such as Locke, the foundation for society lay in the natural law, which was written by God but potentially accessible to all adult humans through reason.

Recently the very concept that there could be one legitimate foundation to a just society has been under attack. In addition to the objections from Marxists and relativists, anti-foundationalists or, as some are known, post-modernists, argue that the notion that there could be any basis of legitimacy for a society is linked to a false notion of truth.[4] For these thinkers, nothing in society is permanent–least of all ideas about justice and equality. Philosophers who seek such a foundation, on their view are attempting to escape to a mythical Archimedean point. Post-modernists argue we are all bound by our contingent place in time and space, which itself has no foundation.

If the post-modernists are right, it would be foolish at best to look for foundations to our contemporary controversies. One way to avoid the post-modernist attack would have been to title my book "Philosophical Assumptions of Contemporary Controversies." Indeed, this title would have achieved one of my main goals, to show that the debates over the death penalty and welfare are linked to other more basic issues in society. I have, however, retained the notion that there are in fact philosophical foundations, not just assumptions, to these debates, for two reasons.

First, many of the assumptions that underlie popular positions on the death penalty and welfare are indeed linked to traditional foundationalist theories. The influence of Locke, for instance, on American political culture is well documented, and indeed his theory of the state is at the root of many positions in both controversies that I deal with here. I therefore devote a good deal of time to his approaches to both the death penalty and welfare.

Second, even those theorists who are explicitly opposed to the type of foundations that post-modernists attack are in some sense still foundationalists. Specifically, these theorists still attempt to provide a legitimate just foundation for the state at the same time that they reject natural law and every other type of supra-societal basis for society. In the words of one of these thinkers, John Rawls, on whom the second half of the book focuses in great detail, it is possible to offer a "political not metaphysical" account of the just foundation to a state. For Rawls, the just state can be argued for using the common intuitions that people have to judge our current practices. In his view such an approach leads to a "reflective equilibrium" from which societies can construct a view of justice. Rawls has his historical roots in the work of Rousseau, whose account of the state I also focus on in Part II.

Outline

I have divided the text into two parts. Part I examines the connection between the debate over the death penalty and the philosophical controversy regarding retributive justice. Philosophers who discuss retributive justice are concerned with two questions. First, when should a society punish and why is it justified in doing so? Second, when a society does punish, how much punishment should it inflict? These two questions, I argue, must be answered before any person can advance a coherent argument for or against the death penalty. I argue that the debate over the death penalty breaks down into four basic positions. First, one can argue for the death penalty based on the reasons present in the philosophy of retributivism. This philosophy emphasizes guilt and desert. Second, one can argue against the death penalty for retributivist reasons. Third, one can argue for the death penalty based on reasons rooted in the utilitarian philosophy. These include cost, general deterrence and singular deterrence. Fourth, one can argue against the death penalty for these same reasons.

In Part II, I attempt to connect the controversy over whether there is a right to welfare with the philosophical dispute over distributive justice. Philosophers who discuss distributive justice are concerned with what type of distribution of wealth would exist in a fully just society. I argue that the anti-welfarist position is best understood within the tradition of those who take a libertarian position in the debate over distributive justice. I argue against other interpretations that both John Locke and Robert Nozick serve as exemplars of this tradition. In addition, I show that welfarist arguments are best understood in connection to the work of Jean-Jacques Rousseau and John Rawls. I argue throughout Part II that the welfare question cannot be fully understood without an exploration of the ultimate justification of the state and the implications such a justification would have on the way property and wealth are distributed in the just society.

Notes

1   This is true despite the fact that Socrates needed to be "coerced" into a discussion of justice with his interlocutors in *The Republic*.
2   See my "From Liberalism to the End of Juridical Language: An Examination of the Early Marx's Jurisprudence," in A. Sarat and P. Ewick, *Studies in Law, Politics, and Society* (Vol. 18, 1998, Greenwich, CT: JAI Press).
3   B. Williams, *Morality: An Introduction to Ethics* (New York: Harper Collins, 1971).
4   See R. Rorty, *Contingency, Irony, and Solidarity* (Cambridge: Cambridge University Press, 1989).

PART I
THE DEATH PENALTY AND PUNISHMENT

1   Introduction to Part I: The Death Penalty and Punishment

The focus of Part I of this book will be on how the philosophical debate over the justification of punishment underlies the current controversy over capital punishment. Inquiries into justifications of punishment come under the heading of "retributive" justice. Although the theory known as retributivism forms only one of many justifications of punishment, this section is broadly concerned with exploring various conceptions of retributive justice. This general inquiry is essential to understanding the assumptions on both sides of the capital punishment question. I begin by examining the ways in which most people discuss the death penalty. I suggest that one's emotional reaction to the issue can be linked to his or her identification with either the criminal or the victim. Those who focus on the punishment the criminal will receive often feel empathy. In contrast, those who focus on the crime that has been committed and the violence experienced by victims often desire vengeance.

Next, I examine revenge as a justification for punishment. While revenge is often offered as a reason for punishment by allusions to the biblical *lex talionis*–"an eye for an eye, a tooth for a tooth"–the justification has been unpopular with philosophers who have examined the view seriously. In the view of many, revenge is a flawed basis for punishment. After examining revenge as a justification for punishment, I will explore the argument that capital punishment is justified because it deters further crimes. The rate of deterrence linked to a particular punishment is often viewed as an objective measure of distributing punishment. This more "scientific" approach would allow us to decide the capital punishment question by examining whether the penalty deterred crime. Here other problems arise. Can justice be linked simply to consequences? Can a penalty as enormous as death be defended by reference not to the crime itself but to the degree to which it affects others?

Next, I examine retributivist approaches to capital punishment, which with their focus on the rightness or wrongness of the crime itself, seem to avoid the

13

problems raised by the questions above. Advocates of this approach argue that the decisions about whether to punish as well as how much to punish must be based solely on what is deserved according to an objective moral standard. The retributivist, however, also faces problems regarding measurement of the proper penalty, especially when the theory is used to defend capital punishment. Nietzsche, among others, has questioned the link between a retributivist view and the motive of revenge.

Before we begin to examine each of these views, it is worthwhile to consider a possible objection to my approach. When I begin a class on punishment and ask students their views on the death penalty, they often present various combinations of the types of reasons I have set out to examine. Often they combine theories or simply state all of these types of reasons at the same time. Perhaps, if we really wanted to begin by examining the way people talk about punishment and the death penalty, it would be sensible to consider some of these hybrid theories.[1] I have not followed this common approach because I want to show that these views are often in contrast with each other. After students are shown that these different types of reasons are often in conflict with each other, they will often begin to defend one of the views discussed below. In addition, when they are asked to prioritize these views, they begin to see that some are more attractive and less flawed than others are. Of course, they disagree about which theories are flawed and why.

I have attempted to present a variety of approaches to the subject and bring out the flaws that accompany them. I have not attempted to prioritize one theory of punishment in the hope that Part I will serve more as a catalyst for conversations about justification than a conclusive argument about whether our society should have the death penalty.

Note

1   For the most developed of these theories see J. Rawls, "Two Concepts of Rules," in J. Feinberg, *Philosophy of Law* (Belmont: Wadsworth, 1995).

2 Revenge, Pity and Empathy: Common Roots of the Death Penalty Debate

Outside the gates of United States maximum-security prisons, where hundreds wait for executions on death row, lies a central battleground in the contemporary controversy over capital punishment. Often, on the eve of an execution, two groups of demonstrators gather within sight of each other. On one side, a rowdy group carries signs expressing their approval of the death penalty. Many carry posters, which cite the ancient law of the Bible, that is, *lex talionis*: "An eye for an eye, a tooth for a tooth." In the minutes leading up to the execution a countdown is begun until the last few seconds are chanted by the death penalty supporters in unison. As the execution is officially announced, cheers erupt from the crowd.

At the same time, another group, quiet and somber, holds a candlelight prayer vigil. These demonstrators often sing Christian hymns and ask forgiveness from God. They lament the lack of mercy in our system. If asked about their views many in this crowd would focus on the cruelty of the actual process of putting someone to death. They are pensive as the moment of death approaches. Their mood reflects both a desire to forgive the person being executed as well as the system responsible for his or her death. At the moment of execution, they are immersed in tearful prayer.

Often, the decision to join one of these two groups of activists, or indeed to demonstrate at all, depends in large part on whether one empathizes with the victim of a crime committed or with those currently on death row. Many find it easy to identify with those who have been victims of violent crime. Their stories are often told on the evening news and cause many viewers to think "That could be me or a close family member." This fear of being victimized can easily lead to a craving for vengeance. It is perhaps less likely that one would empathize with a violent criminal due to a news broadcast. Although some news stories, books and films have succeeded in bringing out the humanity of those facing execution, television journalists usually describe

15

criminals on death row in impersonal terms. While understanding criminals' lives and the factors that led them to commit violent acts might not lead most people to forgiveness, it could lead to enough empathy to prevent the public from desiring execution.

Many people also begin to empathize with those on death row when they learn of the brutal nature of the execution process. Electrocution, for instance, often causes the eyes to protrude from their sockets before death has been pronounced. The gas chamber completely suffocates its victims. The film *Dead Man Walking* brought to light the psychological cruelty of even the ostensibly humane form of execution, lethal injection.[1]

While most people react emotionally to the death penalty issue, the purpose of this book is to get beyond emotional reactions and ask if the penalty is just. Before we do proceed, however, it is sensible to examine the role, if any, that emotions should play in the punishment process. It is important to examine empathy and revenge, not just because they are major contributors to the public's attitudes about the death penalty, but because they have played a role at the highest levels of legal decision making.

Revenge, Pity and Empathy: The Supreme Court's Rhetoric

The appeal to emotion has been used not just by death penalty demonstrators, but by US Supreme Court Justices in their decisions. Since the mid-1970s, the Supreme Court has held that the death penalty is, in certain forms, constitutional. Between the 1970s and early 1990s, Justice Harold Blackmun joined in several of the decisions to uphold it. In 1994, however, Blackmun dissented from the majority of the court *Callins* vs. *Collins*. Although the petition was denied by the majority of the court, Blackmun broke with past decisions and argued that the death penalty was so overwhelmingly cruel that he had no choice but to rule it unconstitutional. His rhetorical technique is to focus, as do many death penalty protesters, on the horror of the actual punishment. By focusing on the act itself, he has the potential to evoke pity or sympathy, emotions that are helpful to death penalty abolitionists. He details the process of execution at the beginning of his decision:

> On February 23, 1994, at approximately 1:00 A.M., Bruce Edwin Callins will be executed by the State of Texas. Intravenous tubes attached to his arms will carry the instrument of death, a toxic fluid designed specifically for the purpose of killing human beings. The witness, standing a few feet away, will behold Callins, no longer a defendant, an appellant, or a petitioner, but a man, strapped to a gurney, and seconds away from extinction.[2]

Blackmun's horror at the process of execution contributes to the following conclusion: "From this day forward, I no longer shall tinker with the machinery of death . . . I feel morally and intellectually obliged to concede that the death penalty experiment has failed."[3] By focusing on the actual act of putting a human being to death, opponents of the death penalty hope to produce moral and emotional reprehension within the public. Here Blackmun invites the reader to take the position of the witness who is steps from the brutal act of execution. By imagining oneself in such a position, the reader would presumably react with horror or perhaps empathy.

Death penalty supporters also rely on emotional reaction to bolster their cause; however, they focus on the cruel acts of the criminals being executed, hoping to horrify the public into support for the penalty. This horror is at the root of what is perhaps the most commonly invoked argument for the death penalty: the need for revenge. Although the victim cannot feel the satisfaction of revenge, proponents of the family can experience it vicariously. Many supporters of the death penalty often cite the need to protect family members or children as part of their defense for the punishment. It is not a great leap to claim that imagining oneself or one's own loved ones in the position of the victim would lead to an even greater emotional need for vengeance and for a feeling of vindication during the execution of a murderer.

The desire for vengeance, like the call for empathy, is invoked at all levels of the death penalty debate. In a reply to Justice Blackmun's previously cited response to the *Callins* vs. *Collins* petition, Justice Antonin Scalia reinforces the notion that vengeance is perhaps an appropriate reaction when heinous crimes have been committed. Scalia recognizes that by focusing on the act of execution, Blackmun hopes to bring to the surface emotions such as pity that would lead us to an anti-death penalty position. He counters Blackmun and follows the strategy of many death penalty supporters by highlighting the heinousness of certain capital crimes:

> Justice Blackmun begins his statement by describing with poignancy the death by lethal injection. He chooses, as the case in which to make that statement, one of the less brutal of the murders that regularly come before us–the murder of a man ripped by a bullet suddenly and unexpectedly, with no opportunity to prepare himself and his affairs, and left to bleed to death on the floor of a tavern. The death by injection which Justice Blackmun describes looks pretty desirable next to that. It looks even better next to some of the other cases currently before us which Justice Blackmun did not select as the vehicle for his announcement that the death penalty is always unconstitutional–for example, the case of the 11-year-old girl raped by four men and then killed by stuffing her panties down her throat.[4]

Contra Blackmun, Scalia argues here that pity is not the appropriate reaction when criminals are executed, reminding his audience of the brutal acts for which these criminals are often responsible. Despite their differing views on the death penalty issue, both justices rely on a similar rhetorical technique: the invocation of an emotional reaction. Scalia appeals to the need for vengeance in response to a gruesome crime, while Blackmun appeals to pity by concentrating on the heinousness of the penalty itself.

Revenge as a Justification

While appeals to revenge are common, philosophers have often been skeptical of this desire as a valid justification for punishment. The question remains: is the call for revenge a compelling reason for the death penalty? Vengefulness is often a fleeting emotion rather than a principle or a reason. As a result, I will argue, it is of little use in developing a theory of punishment. While for many people revenge is linked to the desire for punishment, I will show that it is of little help in implementing public policy. This is evident if we attempt to conceive of a system of punishment based entirely on vengeance.

As I have noted, many death penalty proponents who want to use revenge as a justification refer to the biblical *lex talionis*: "An eye for an eye, a tooth for a tooth." But consider the difference between biblical law and a view which rests on a personal feeling like revenge. Not everyone feels the same desire for revenge after a crime. Some might feel angry enough to demonstrate outside a prison. Others find themselves feeling pity for a criminal, perhaps even asking for mercy on his or her behalf. The principle of "an eye for an eye," however, seems to offer a clear objective guideline for appropriate punishment. While *lex talionis* is often cited to support a victim's call for vengeance, if one takes the principle seriously, its dictates are bound to conflict with the feelings of victims. At times, in fact, *lex talionis* demands restraint. While in some instances of grave harm, but not murder, vengeful victims might call for the death penalty, *lex talionis* in fact prohibits it. According to this biblical law, murder deserves death, but other crimes do not. *Lex talionis* is therefore not a justification for revenge and indeed at times opposes this emotion.

While I do not want to argue that *lex talionis* should be embraced, consistent principles do offer a better basis for punishment than personal vengeful feelings. The philosopher John Locke demonstrates the erratic nature of revenge in his *Second Treatise on Government*.[5] As Locke sees it, the desire for revenge depends in large part on one's individual personality and circumstances. For two reasons this would result in major inconsistencies in punishment. First, the decision regarding guilt or innocence would be biased by one's relationship to the victim. One who has been wronged, according to Locke, would often be quicker to pronounce an individual, perhaps an innocent individual, guilty than would an unbiased and emotionally detached judge. Second, the degree of punishment people felt a criminal deserved would depend in large part on their proximity to the crime. The victim and her family would probably demand an immense punishment, while those who did not know the victim would be less likely to do so.

Locke attempts to demonstrate his point by examining what life would be like without government, or in his words, in a "state of nature." Locke argues that in such a state, individuals would have rights similar to the ones they have now in liberal democracies. People would own property, he argues, and recognize that each individual has a right not to be harmed. He argues that the ungoverned state of nature would only differ from our society in that there would be no organized system of punishment. There would be no courts to decide cases and no police to enforce the laws. According to Locke, law would exist in the state of nature. In fact, everyone would be aware of the law and sincerely attempt to uphold it. Despite the best of intentions, however, he argues, emotions would actually dominate when deciding upon punishment. In Locke's view, the result of decisions tinged by revenge would be violent anarchy. Disputes and crimes, which could otherwise be handled with minimal harm, would result in continual sentences of death carried out by angry individuals and mobs. Because people would settle disputes entrapped by feelings, vengeance would become the impetus for all social interaction, resulting in a constant state of war.

As Locke sees it, the threat of such an outcome would lead all persons in such a society to give up their power to make decisions concerning the law. They would recognize that a state represented by objective judges could enforce law better than individuals motivated by passions. The point here is not only that a punitive system based on revenge would be unfair but that such a system would be unworkable.

One of the main reasons why a revenge-based system would fail is that punishments would be given out in an erratic manner. The principle that "like crimes must be treated in like manner" could simply not be upheld. Two people could commit the same crimes but receive completely different punishments based solely on the temperament of the person deciding the punishment. If the principle of consistency in punishment is to be upheld, Locke concludes, we must abandon revenge as a justification for punishment.

In addition to creating inconsistent punishments, relying on revenge could serve to justify existing prejudices. Throughout American history, all-white juries have convicted black defendants charged with capital crimes at much higher rates than white defendants charged with the same crimes. Leaving aside the question of whether this statistic alone is grounds to abolish the death penalty within our legal system (an issue I will discuss at the end of this section), consider the consequences of a system based entirely on emotion. In a society in which people often identify with groups who share the same skin color, vengeance might vary depending on the race of a jury and the race of defendants. For whites, the desire for revenge against an African American who has been accused of a crime might be higher than the desire for revenge against a white person accused of the same crime. To sum up, four problems exist with using revenge as a justification for punishment. First, it is often unreliable in determining whom to punish. Second, it can be excessive. Third, it is erratic. Fourth, it can be racist.

Notes

1   For an expanded discussion of this film see A. Sarat, "The Cultural Life of Capital Punishment: Responsibility and Representation in Dead Man Walking and Last Dance," in *The Killing State: Capital Punishment in Law, Politics and Culture* (Oxford: Oxford University Press, 1999). Sarat examines the role responsibility plays in *Dead Man Walking*.
2   *Callins* vs. *Collins*, No. 93–7054 (1994) (Blackmun, J., dissenting). Reprinted in R.M. Baird and S.E. Rosenbaum (eds), *Punishment and the Death Penalty* (Amherst, NY: Prometheus Books, 1995) p. 241.
3   Ibid.
4   *Callins* vs. *Collins*, No. 93–7054 (1994) (Scalia, A., concurring). Reprinted in R.M. Baird and S.E. Rosenbaum (eds), *Punishment and the Death Penalty*, p. 241.
5   I explore Locke's view of property in much greater depth in Part II of this book on welfare and distributive justice.

3   Emotion Defended

While I have argued against revenge, some might still want to defend the importance of emotion in justifying punishment. Some have argued that emotional reactions are appropriate in facing the violent circumstances that normally accompany capital cases. It is a problem that our society is so accustomed to violence that it no longer feels a sense of outrage upon hearing about a murder. It could be argued that if people do not feel the need for revenge when watching the evening news report, they do not have the correct emotional reaction.

This view is flawed, however, at least as applied to punishment. While we might agree that people should react emotionally to tragedies, notice that this claim assumes that some emotions are appropriate in certain situations. The assumption that certain responses are appropriate in certain circumstances implies that we cannot simply trust emotion without evaluating it. Therefore the punishment debate must be argued in terms of what the just emotional reaction to heinous crimes should be. The debate then moves from a discussion of facts about how people actually react to certain situations to an exploration of how they should react. We must search for a consistent and objective criterion for punishment in order to avert the problems of inconsistency brought out by Locke.

Still, there are other defenses of emotions as a basis for punishment. Perhaps one might deny that it is possible to actually overcome our emotions in developing an objective standard. As I have stated before, racist juries, although claiming to judge objectively, have often imposed their own personal emotional reactions in judging capital crimes. Although people often claim to act based on justice, the term "justice" can serve as a cover which masks revenge. It is actually more honest, it could be claimed, for people to simply admit that their actions are based on emotions.

Two initial responses are appropriate here. First, to claim that most people would not base their actions on an objective standard of justice or to say that most people would not employ such a standard in explaining their actions (think of the protesters outside the gates) is not to say that there is not an objective and just answer to the death penalty controversy. People often hold false opinions in regard to science. How many people can actually explain quantum mechanics? It is equally possible that they lack the proper explanations for or against the death penalty.

Second, by saying that a particular solution to a philosophical question is just, one implies that it is also practical. A conception of justice that is incompatible with an individual's capacity to act is obviously flawed. To borrow a popular phrase in philosophy, "Ought implies can." If a particular conception of punishment would inevitably collapse into personal bias or vengeance–and, therefore, inconsistency and impracticality–it is clearly a flawed conception.

While most people rely on emotions in deciding which types of punishments they view as just, they would be appalled by the consequences of an entire system of punishment based on vengeance. Their acknowledgement of the instability and inconsistency of such a punishment would cause them to seek a more consistent system of justice. It is another question whether or not it is possible to implement such a system. In fact, as we shall see in Chapter 7, some philosophers have argued that despite our attempts to overcome our vengeful instincts, we are doomed to fail. In the view of Fredrick Nietzsche, punishment, especially consistent punishment, is inherently vengeful. First, however, I shall consider the methods that have commonly been used to create a consistent system of punishment. I will demonstrate that even a consistent system is no guarantee of a just system.

4   General Deterrence

One of the most popular justifications for the death penalty is general deterrence –the notion that it deters others from committing serious crimes. In fact, both advocates and opponents of the death penalty often focus solely on the question of whether or not the death penalty prevents crime. There is research to support both sides of the question. Advocates of the death penalty point to studies suggesting that highly publicized executions deter some criminals from committing capital crimes. Specifically, they cite data showing that crime has decreased in states in which the death penalty has been instituted.[1] Opponents claim that the data is inconclusive. Some have even argued that the death penalty incites crime. They maintain that the high level of publicity received by some death-row inmates sometimes inspires pathological attention seekers to commit crimes for which there would otherwise be no motivation.

Although opinions differ about the veracity of these conclusions, all of those who rely on general deterrence data share a common assumption: the impact that the death penalty has on society at large is relevant to a decision about how to punish an individual who is accused of a crime. On this view, the actual act carried out by the accused, and the character and personal history of the accused, are consequential when a decision about punishment is being made, only to the degree to which they affect general deterrence. Despite the seemingly intrinsic importance of these factors, if they have no effect on the actions of potential criminals they are irrelevant. Instead, the sole criterion used to determine the appropriate punishment is the degree to which that punishment affects the actions of others.

Proponents of general deterrence claim that this principle is superior to revenge. Indeed, the general deterrence explanation seems more 'scientific' and avoids two problems we found with revenge in the previous section. First, the general deterrence theory does not encourage the populace to fixate on the horror of the crime but provides them with a constructive response to it: the reduction of future criminal behavior. Whereas a policy based on revenge responds to crime by imposing suffering on the person being punished regardless of the benefit to society, deterrence ensures that society benefits from what otherwise might be a purely destructive act.

Second, the problem of inconsistency seems to be avoided. While the desire for revenge is sporadic and dependent on the individuals who have been affected by a crime, the principle of deterrence seems to provide an objective and consistent means for determining punishment. Rather than relying on emotions, the general deterrence principle rests on facts. Advocates of this approach ask simply: will the punishment deter? These theorists claim they are able to provide a consistent method for determining the degree of punishment. Social scientists could determine which particular punishments deter and which do not, and legislatures could respond accordingly. Deterrence seems, then, to offer an objective and consistent criterion for punishment.

However, this appearance is deceptive. Consider the following example. John, an extremely popular political leader, is accused of murder. Most people consider this leader to have a great deal of integrity and therefore believe he is innocent. Releasing him, even if he is in fact guilty, would therefore not set a bad precedent; the public would believe that an innocent man had been released. Further, opinions are so staunchly in favour of acquitting John that his conviction would spark widespread rioting and civil unrest. In such a case, rather than deterring crime, punishment would incite it. On the grounds of general deterrence, it would seem that regardless of John's guilt, he should be released. Here a concern with guilt is replaced by a consideration of society's overall well-being. If a common citizen committed a similar crime and his conviction would serve to deter further crime, punishment would seem to be warranted. This creates an inconsistency in punishment. Although both acts are alike, differing societal reactions would result in different punishments.

General deterrence could also justify punishing the innocent in certain cases. Consider a case in which a police officer was accused of beating a member of an ethnic minority group. If such an accusation took place in an atmosphere of already strained relations between this group and the police, the acquittal of the officer could cause even further erosion of trust in the police and perhaps an increase in law-breaking. Failure to convict in this case would increase rather than prevent crime. Regardless of the guilt or innocence of the particular officer, punishment is justified here on general deterrence grounds.

In both these cases the principle of general deterrence would necessitate that actual innocence or guilt be ignored. As a result, unequal punishments could be justified. Although, at first, general deterrence seemed to be a less arbitrary criterion for punishment than vengeance, on closer reflection it too seems to be inconsistent.

Some advocates of general deterrence might argue that consistency need not be sacrificed by this principle. They might claim that consistent punishments are necessary to build societal respect for the law, even at the occasional cost of short-term deterrence. Perhaps, they might argue, it is more important to maintain long-term respect for the law through consistent punishments than to ensure that every individual punishment deters crime.

Even if we were to grant that a policy based on general deterrence could maintain consistent punishments, another significant problem exists with the principle. Namely, general deterrence seems to allow for punishments that are excessive. Consider the following example. An urban area is having immense problems with traffic caused in large part by illegal parking. These traffic problems do not merely inconvenience commuters, but they interfere with the passage of emergency vehicles, which results in lost lives. Desperate to improve emergency services and thus save lives, the city could announce that parking violations would be met with a punishment of five years' imprisonment. Although the punishment is overly harsh, it would certainly serve to deter parking violations completely. Even if one illegal parker had to be imprisoned to serve as an example to society at large, from the perspective of general deterrence this sacrifice might be justified by the number of additional lives that would be saved by swiftly moving emergency vehicles. After all, while one person would lose five years of freedom, that person's punishment would result in lives being saved. An advocate of general deterrence could justify this excessive punishment.

To sum up, there are three potential problems with general deterrence. First, it risks treating similar crimes differently because of the social milieu in which they are committed. Second, it leaves open the possibility of punishing innocents and freeing the guilty. In the case of the celebrity politician's murder trial and the police brutality trial, the question of guilt was superseded by a concern for general deterrence. Third, it may allow for excessive punishments. In the case of the illegal parker, the death penalty could have been justified because it deterred dangerous parking situations. I will return to consider some defenses of general deterrence in a later exploration of utilitarianism. First, however, we will investigate some theoretical alternatives to general deterrence as a means for evaluating punishment and the legitimacy of the death penalty.

Note

1   See Sowell, "Defenders of Murderers Spring into Action," *Manchester Union Leader*, December 13, 1994. Also see DiIulio, "Retrieve the Death Penalty from Symbolism," *American Enterprise*, May/June 1995. Both are reprinted in P. Winters (ed.), *The Death Penalty* (San Diego, CA: Greenhaven, 1997).

5 Singular Deterrence and Rehabilitation

As we have seen, those following the principle of general deterrence determine the degree of punishment for a crime based on the impact this punishment will have on others not involved in the crime. In contrast to general deterrence, the principles of both singular deterrence and rehabilitation focus on the individual who has committed a crime. While both approaches offer differing frameworks for evaluating capital punishment, neither focuses on the impact punishment has on others. I begin this section by distinguishing general from singular deterrence. I then explore why singular deterrence theory is often seen to justify the death penalty and then explore whether or not singular deterrence can overcome the problems associated with general deterrence. I end by considering the related justification of rehabilitation.

Singular deterrence is the principle that punishment is justified because it prevents recidivism. While general deterrence based punishment on the impact it would have on society at large, singular deterrence is based solely on preventing the individual accused of a crime from violating the law again. As a result, in theory this seems to be a fairer punishment than general deterrence. As we have seen, punishment policies based on general deterrence focus on factors beyond the actions of the person to be punished resulting at times in unequal and unfair punishments. Singular deterrence, however, links the punishment of the accused to his or her own future actions.

The question of whether or not the death penalty is justified on singular deterrence grounds is controversial. Capital punishment obviously deters the individual who has committed a crime from doing so again. This leads certain defenders of singular deterrence to argue for the penalty. Other supporters of singular deterrence who oppose the death penalty, however, counter that life imprisonment could offer the same guarantee of society's safety. They argue that it is much more difficult to commit crimes from behind bars. Proponents of the death penalty respond that such punishment gives the prisoner opportunity to kill during incarceration. They argue that the lives of other inmates as well as prison guards are put at risk when those convicted of murder continue to live. Like the principal of general deterrence, the principle of singular deterrence leaves the question of capital punishment open to debate.

Regardless of the way singular deterrence is applied to capital punishment, the question remains as to whether this principle can overcome the problems associated with general deterrence. We found two major flaws with general deterrence in the previous section. First, it made guilt unessential in regard to punishment. Second, it allowed for excessive punishment. Singular deterrence seems to avoid the first of these problems. If the point of singular deterrence is to prevent a particular individual who has committed a crime from doing so again, it would seem to be counter-productive to punish an innocent. After all, if someone has not committed a crime, why would there be reason to assume she would do so in the future? Consider, however, the problem that would arise if it became possible to predict that individuals would commit crimes in the future even though they had not yet done so. According to the principle of singular deterrence, we would seem to be justified in incarcerating these people in order to prevent them from carrying out the crimes. Although we might not use the term "punishment" because the person had not done anything wrong, we would effectively be detaining them in much the same way as if they had committed a crime.[1] If the crime in question was murder, perhaps an execution would be warranted on the grounds of singular deterrence. Punishments would serve the same purpose of deterring future crime despite the fact that in one case an individual was guilty of a crime, whereas in the other the person was innocent of any actual wrongdoing.

Those who wished to defend singular deterrence against these charges might argue that such prediction is not possible at the current time. We could perhaps predict some future behavior, but we are by no means capable of certain prediction. In the future, however, genetics and behavioral psychology might make such prediction possible from birth. If such advances were made, what would prevent an advocate of singular deterrence from demanding the imprisonment of some innocent children who could be predicted to commit crimes in the future? Regardless of our current capacities, singular deterrence opens the door to the possibility of using social science and genetics to determine punishment. Those who will be targeted might not be guilty of a crime before punishment, but they would become guilty if they were not punished in time. Guilt would become just a matter of timing in singular deterrence terms.

The second problem of general deterrence, that it justifies excessive punishment, might also seem to be resolved by singular deterrence. We saw that general deterrence could lead to an excessive use of the death penalty because it could be seen to influence large numbers of people in certain vital policy situations. With singular deterrence, of course, punishment is based on the actions or future actions of an individual without regard to the effect punishment will have on the society as a whole. However, this difference does not eliminate the risk of excessive punishment. While it is clear that the death penalty would prevent those who murder from doing so again, it would also prevent those who have committed lesser offenses, such as theft, from murdering. If singular deterrence is the only criterion for punishment, why not consider the death penalty for all crimes? In fact, it might be argued that those who commit petty crimes at a young age are likely to commit more serious crimes later in life, so they should be killed to prevent these crimes. While some proponents of singular deterrence might argue against such a policy by claiming previous crimes are evidence only of the propensity to commit the same crimes in the future, these proponents face the same attack we saw in the previous paragraph: future developments in genetics and behavioral psychology could differentiate between those who might commit serious future crimes and those who will never move beyond petty thievery.

In response to the accusation that their principle could lead to excessive punishment, defenders of singular deterrence could argue that for most petty thieves, the threat of prison would be enough to deter future crimes, and the death penalty would be unnecessary. Here, however, we are led back to a problem that plagued advocates of revenge. In cases in which one person could be deterred by the threat of a prison term but another would not, singular deterrence would seem to allow for inconsistent punishments for individuals who had committed exactly the same crime. In fact, if we use singular deterrence as our criterion, some crimes might receive the death penalty while other offenders could be completely let off. Consider the case of a person who makes a conscious decision to kill once. If there was a scientific guarantee she would not do so again, it could be argued by a proponent of singular deterrence that there were no grounds for punishment. On the other hand, a person who committed the same crime but would do so again could be given the death penalty.

The same problems that accompanied general deterrence also arise with singular deterrence. First, the principle of singular deterrence could be used to target those who have the propensity to commit crime but have not already done anything wrong. Second, it could justify excessive and inconsistent punishments.

Rehabilitation

Rehabilitation has been perhaps as popular a justification of punishment as deterrence has. In fact, many American penal institutions are still called "Corrections" institutions. Advocates of this approach have argued that rehabilitation is a much more humane and merciful justification for punishment than either revenge or deterrence. Perhaps in an attempt to support this argument, in the mid-twentieth century, proponents of this approach dubbed their theory the "Humanitarian" theory of punishment. Humanitarian theorists have been fierce opponents of the death penalty for obvious reasons. If the purpose of punishment is rehabilitation, capital punishment clearly cannot accomplish this goal; the death penalty results in the end of life, not the reformation of one's personality. Unlike the other views we have examined, rehabilitation leaves no flexibility on the death penalty issue.

There seem at first to be several advantages to rehabilitation over previous views. First, those supporting the rehabilitation principle recognize that a method of treatment is necessary to prevent further crime. Except in the case of the death penalty, punishment alone is often not enough to deter future crime. This treatment can be personally tailored to an individual's needs, taking into account the specific reasons and influences that led an individual to commit a crime in the first place. While the principles of revenge, general deterrence and singular deterrence are concerned merely with protecting and pleasing society at large, rehabilitation has the benefit of serving the needs of some of society's most troubled individuals.

While the rehabilitation approach might seem humane, its opponents have argued that it fails to provide a justification for punishment in the first place. While rehabilitation might be a good answer to the question of how those convicted of crimes should be treated, it does not necessarily explain why society is justified in punishing in the first place.

In his book *God in the Dock*, the theologian and writer C.S. Lewis argues that rehabilitation is a flawed justification for punishment because it leaves no room for the concept of a "just" punishment.[2] In fact, Lewis argues, rehabilitation and deterrence share common flaws. Despite the title of the theory, Lewis writes, "The 'humanity' which it claims is a dangerous illusion and disguises the possibility of cruelty and injustice without end."[3] The humanitarian theory demands that we cease to see individuals as having both rights and responsibility. As a result, the theory, he claims, transforms individuals into "patients" who need to be cured. Under the veil of a cure, any punishment could be inflicted, he claims, regardless of whether or not it is excessive or just. Central to his theory is the claim that all punishments that are just must also be deserved. By treating criminals as patients, Lewis argues, the theory leaves no room for this type of moral evaluation. "The Humanitarian theory" therefore "removes from Punishment the concept of Desert . . . But the concept of Desert is the only connecting link between punishment and justice. It is only as deserved or undeserved that a sentence can be just or unjust." Because the Humanitarian theory as well as deterrence theories are concerned with changing future action, they ignore questions of justice in punishment. In Lewis's words, there is no sense in talking about a "just deterrent" or a "just cure." We demand of a deterrent not whether it is just but whether it will deter. We demand of a cure not whether it is just but whether it succeeds. Thus when we cease to consider what the criminal deserves and consider only what will cure him or deter others, we have tacitly removed him from the sphere of justice altogether; instead of a person, a subject of right, we now have a mere object, a patient, a "case."[4]

Since effectiveness in punishment is independent from desert, the humanitarian theory, like deterrence, could lead to excessive or light sentencing. While the death penalty would never be justified, consider again the case of the petty thief. Even if the thief had only stolen an item such as a chocolate bar, she might be detained for years on the grounds that she had not been rehabilitated. Imagine that after thirty years of therapy, doctors decided she had not been cured. On the other hand, consider the previous example of the person who killed once but would never do so again. On the humanitarian theory, such a person might have been only temporarily sick, perhaps only sick at the time the murder was carried out. Since he would need no further therapy, he should be released.

Perhaps it could be argued that although rehabilitation, singular deterrence and general deterrence are all flawed principles for evaluating punishment, one of these principles offers the best alternative to revenge. After all, at least each provides a clear standard for judging punishment and for evaluating the use of the death penalty. Many theorists have actually claimed that given the choice between deterrence, rehabilitation and revenge, the former two are preferable simply because they are not the latter. According to author Richard Nygaard, the abandonment of both rehabilitation and deterrence as justifications of punishment "leaves only retribution. Revenge. The ultimate payback. As a retributory tool, death works wonderfully. The desire for revenge is the dark secret in us all." According to Nygaard, revenge is the only real reason one could find in defense of the death penalty if one rejects general deterrence and rehabilitation.[5] Since revenge can never justify a punishment, Nygaard argues the death penalty is unjust.

Despite the fact that Nygaard equates revenge with "retribution," the latter has actually been the basis for a theory that many believe avoids the problems of vengeance, deterrence and rehabilitation. Among those theorists is Lewis, who writes, "I urge a return to the traditional or retributive theory not solely, not even primarily, in the interests of society, but in the interests of the criminal." For Lewis, like other retributive theorists, a theory based on desert and justice can be distinguished from deterrence theories, rehabilitation and revenge. The theory has led to differing positions on the death penalty and brings up new problems. We turn to this theory in the next section.

Notes

1   I owe this point to Nick Schretzman.
2   Lewis, "The Humanitarian Theory of Punishment," in J. Feinberg, *Reason and Responsibility* (Belmont: Wadsworth, 1993), p. 432.
3   Ibid.
4   Ibid.
5   Nygaard, *Vengeance is Mine, America*, as quoted in P. Winters (ed.), *The Death Penalty* (San Diego, CA: Greenhaven, 1997), p. 110. Nygaard uses this reasoning to argue against the death penalty. His theory is of interest here, however, because he believes rehabilitation, deterrence and revenge are jointly exhaustive justifications of punishment.

6   Retribution

The suggestion that proponents of general deterrence could be led to support punishing innocents and in some situations justify the death penalty for innocent people is morally objectionable. The same is true of the claim that the general deterrence principle could legitimize excessive punishments for the guilty. Many people view it as simply morally wrong to punish the innocent or impose overly harsh punishments on the guilty. Retributivists argue that these strong intuitions against excessive or undeserved punishment strongly support the notion that punishments must be deserved. The popular phrase that the "punishment must fit the crime" captures some of what the retributivist means by "desert." But whereas this phrase implies that certain crimes always should be accompanied by certain punishments regardless of who has committed them, the notion of desert can account for individual circumstances in a way that "fit" does not.[1] For instance, the retributivist can recognize that certain personal circumstances mitigate against the punishments that seem to fit–someone who steals bread for food could, on retributivist grounds, deserve less punishment than someone who committed the same crime for fun. On the retributivist view, the notion that punishments must be morally deserved should have a large role in any legitimate theory of punishment. The retributivist's emphasis on desert leads to the conclusion that a theory of punishment should be based in a theory of morality. In the retributivist view, the effect of punishment is irrelevant. Regardless of the consequences to society or the individual, only punishments that are morally permissible should be implemented by society.

While this theory might have a basis in moral feelings and intuitions, retributivists argue that actual moral responses are not subjective and fleeting. They contend that a feeling of revulsion is appropriate in the face of an excessive punishment because such a punishment is, objectively, morally wrong. In their view, some punishments are morally deserved while others are not. It might seem logical for this theory to bring us back to the arguments for revenge and pity that we discarded at the beginning of this Part. After all, revenge and pity are often called "moral reactions" by those who have them. Further, the terms "revenge" and "retribution" are often used as synonyms;

surely, then, retributivists must fall into the same type of inconsistency in which proponents of revenge find themselves trapped. However, this is not the case. Most retributivists make a strong distinction between revenge and retribution. The contemporary philosopher Ernest van den Haag explains that

> revenge is a private matter, a wish to "get even" with another one feels they have been injured by regardless of whether or not what the person did was legal. Unlike revenge, retribution is legally threatened beforehand for an act prohibited by law . . . The desire for revenge is a personal feeling. Retribution is a legally imposed social institution.[2]

Here van den Haag links retribution to legality. This view has an advantage over the type of vengeance that dominates Locke's state of nature in that here punishment cannot be based on a temporary whim. The desire for vengeance might be strong immediately following a crime, but the inherent distance and objectivity that comes with legal punishment would temper such a desire.

However, we must remember that though retributive laws might provide a measure of distance and objectivity, they are not shielded from the influence of emotions. As I mentioned earlier, citizens with a deep-seated need for revenge could vote candidates who support the death penalty into office. For some, such desire lasts a lifetime and contributes to the institution of criminal law. These laws are not magically purified of their emotional impetus; legislated vengeful punishment is still vengeful punishment. In addition, at times when the public's desire for revenge is particularly high–during a crime wave, for instance–legislatures could institute private whim at a public level. Retributivists need to do more than claim that punishments are carried out by public institutions to distinguish retribution from revenge. Namely, they need to demonstrate more clearly that some moral reactions are appropriate responses to certain crimes. This task is especially necessary for retributivists who want to argue that the theory justifies the death penalty.

Perhaps the most ancient system of ensuring proportionate measurement comes from the principle of *lex talionis*, which we previously distinguished from revenge. As many commentators have pointed out, this principle was meant to limit punishment during a time when assault might be met with the death penalty through vicious means. While *lex talionis* is a retributive principle and not simply an emotion, in contemporary times this principle has been condemned as excessive. Martin Luther King famously commented that an "eye for an eye, a tooth for a tooth" would "leave both men blind." King's statement implies that the theory offers an excessive principle of punishment. Although van den Haag argues that retributivism necessitates the death penalty, he rejects the biblical formula of *lex talionis* as vengeful and excessive. He is therefore left in a tricky situation. As he himself admits, "retribution is hard to define. It is harder still to determine the punishments that should be exacted by 'just deserts' once the lex talionis is abandoned." Essentially, van den Haag faces the task of justifying the death penalty without recourse to either revenge or the proportional system of biblical law.

In an attempt to construct this justification, he argues that the most serious punishments are the morally correct reactions to the most serious crimes. In his view, to give a lenient punishment for a serious crime would result in a trivialization of the offence itself. Just as it would be outrageous to give the death penalty for parking violations, in van den Haag's view it would be similarly wrong to allow a murderer to merely serve time in prison. As he explains:

> One may well argue that human life is cheapened when murderers, instead of being executed, are imprisoned as pickpockets are . . . The discontinuity between murder and other crimes should be underlined by the death penalty, not blurred by punishing murderers as one punishes thieves. Murder is not so trifling an offense.[3]

The death penalty, according to van den Haag, is the most serious penalty a society has the ability to use. To give a murderer anything less would be to "trivialize" the offense by placing it on the same level as lesser offenses like thievery.

Anti-Death Penalty Retributivism

While van den Haag argues that a belief in retributivism justifies the death penalty as a punishment for murder (he also does not rule out the death penalty for other serious crimes such as rape, or as a just punishment for minors), others argue that retributivism actually leads to an anti-death penalty position. Several intuitions support this position. First, it is not clear why death must be the most serious punishment to which society has recourse. If life in prison were the most serious punishment, other less serious offenses would deserve less time in prison. Life in prison would certainly not be a punishment comparable to two years in prison. If van den Haag's point is that the death penalty is necessary because it is a different type of penalty than prison, he seems to have a practical problem. While van den Haag only mentions the death penalty and prison, there are certainly more than two different degrees of seriousness in crime. Accommodating a view that demanded different types of punishment for different degrees of crime would take an incredibly creative system of punishment. Short of this, however, it is not clear why a punishment less severe than death could not be the most serious punishment reserved for the most serious crimes.

The second means of support for a retributivist position that is anti-death penalty comes from the common perception that the death penalty is cruel. On this view, made prominent in a Supreme Court decision we will investigate in Chapter 12, the penalty of death is excessive in all cases and thus never deserved. The fact that something is cruel, anti-death penalty retributivists argue, is an indication that it is wrong. Proponents of this view focus on the nature of the punishment of death, which has always involved pain. They argue that a humane system of punishment would never call for the deliberate infliction of pain on a human being. Such arguments have provoked most American states to investigate the possibility of introducing a painless death penalty. After failing to do so with the electric chair and the gas chamber, many states have moved towards lethal injection. These "reforms" are controversial, and some anti-death penalty theorists have argued that even the smaller amount of pain that accompanies lethal injection is cruel and therefore not deserved.

Advocates of a retributivist anti-death approach also point out that there is a particular cruelty in making the convicted wait in prison while knowing that they will be executed at some point. Indeed, this process has often driven death-row inmates to insanity. Some pro-death penalty advocates have pointed out that this process could be made less cruel if executions were carried out more quickly after trial, because the torment inmates face during the waiting period would be eliminated. The anti-death penalty retributivist can offer two responses to this claim. First, the accused will face the psychological pressure of knowing he could possibly be executed throughout the duration of the trial. As some capital trials last for extended periods of time this torment could be substantial. Second, the anti-death retributivist would argue that the justice system in the process of speeding up execution would need to eliminate appeals. While such a policy might relieve some psychological pressure, it would inflict too great a cost on the retributivist obligation to ensure that only the guilty are executed.

Retributivism and Related Philosophical Problems

Regardless of one's view on the death penalty at this point, it might be objected that the retributivist approach to punishment is fundamentally flawed. After all, this Part began by rejecting vengeance because it seemed impossible to base a consistent system of punishment on this principle. Perhaps the same is true for the retributivist theory. While both pro-death penalty and anti-death penalty retributivists appeal to desert as a basis for determining punishment, this seems to be the extent of their agreement. They disagree about what actually is morally deserved. The root of this dispute lies at the foundation of one of the largest questions of philosophy: what is the basis for morality?

The large divide over public issues could lead many to the conclusion that there simply is no answer to the moral question of what crimes deserve what punishments and that therefore retributivist theory is not practical. After all, it could be argued that the inability of US citizens to come to a consensus on the death penalty issue proves that there is no answer. According to this objection to retributivism–based in the theory of moral relativism–any view of punishment which is linked to a moral dispute should be dismissed as useless.[4] There is reason, however, to think the retributivist theory is still viable, despite the seeming uncertainty raised by the relativist objection. There are disputes over issues in which one party is simply wrong. For instance, it is a widely held belief that the common cold is caused by cold, despite scientific evidence to the contrary. Why, then, could we not also conclude that when it comes to principles of punishment, that some simply have an incorrect morality?

A more sophisticated critic of retributivism could claim that even if there is a truth of the matter in regard to morality, this truth is of little value in reaching a consensus about a theory of punishment. The mere fact that so many people disagree about moral truth makes it very hard to implement public policy based on one version of the truth, however true. Despite the fact that the public is divided over the overall morality of the death penalty, there is considerable agreement about whether the punishment is appropriate in certain extreme circumstances. After all, the flaws that we found with excessive punishment in the general deterrence section rested on the assumption that the great majority of people would agree that the death penalty is not appropriate for all crimes.

While the question of whether the death penalty is ever deserved is certainly controversial, there is agreement when it comes to other forms of punishment. For instance, the great majority of people would oppose releasing mass murderers with no punishment. Similarly the great majority of people would reject a very severe punishment for a petty crime, such as life imprisonment for pickpocketing. Perhaps the fact that there is widespread consensus at the extremes of the spectrum of crime and punishment is enough to suggest that retributivism offers the best way to determine punishment. This broad consensus, the retributivist could argue, could serve as the basis for a theory of punishment based in desert. Viewed in the context of underlying agreement, disagreement about what punishment is deserved in specific cases could be framed by retributivist theory. Punishment controversies would then not be seen as evidence of a flaw in retributivism, but rather a discussion within a retributivist framework.

The Assumption of Free Will

Critics of rehabilitation and deterrence claim these theories leave no role for the responsibility of the criminal. Still, the notion of responsibility, essential in the retributivist theory, is not itself without controversy. Specifically, in order to claim that people are responsible for their actions, it is necessary to assume that they acted of their own free will.

Consider the case of an individual who was physically forced to pick up a knife and stab an innocent person. In this case, the individual had no control over the stabbing despite the fact that the knife might have been physically in his hand. It would therefore be nonsensical to find the individual who was forced responsible for the crime.

On a related note, the law seems to incorporate the retributivist notion of responsibility in the principle of *mens rea*, literally "guilty mind." On this view, it is necessary to establish sanity to find someone responsible and therefore guilty. If one can prove a defendant insane, then this defendant cannot be punished. According to this principle, common in the law, a defendant could not be found both guilty and insane. In our system, those who are judged to be insane yet commit criminal acts are usually sent to be treated medically and rehabilitated. We examined an argument in the section on rehabilitation against treating all criminals as patients in need of a cure; in the case of the criminally insane however, even critics of rehabilitation might find this approach appropriate.

While treating, not punishing, the insane because they are not responsible is accepted by many, some philosophers have argued that no people at any time act of their own free will. These philosophers–determinists–argue that people's actions are the result of forces outside their own control. I might believe that when I wake up in the morning and go to work, it is the result of the fact that I have decided to go, but according to determinist theories this impression is mistaken. Instead, determinists would claim that my social surroundings or upbringing, combined with certain biological or genetic factors, have caused me to make this decision. The question remains: If determinism is true and no one has free will can one still be responsible for one's actions? According to theorists known as "incompatabilists," the notion of responsibility rests entirely on free will. In the same way that the insane are judged not to choose their actions and therefore are not found to be responsible, incompatabilists argue that if no one has free will, then no one is responsible for his or her actions.

Even if the claims of determinists are true, some philosophers have argued that it is still possible to find individuals responsible and thus retain the retributivist theory. These thinkers are often referred to as "compatabilists." According to one compatabilist, Robert Nozick, the appropriate amount of retributive punishment can be determined by multiplying the moral seriousness of the crime and the degree to which the individual being punished is responsible for the crime.[5] At first glance, it would seem that if the determinists are correct, the amount of responsibility would be zero and therefore no punishment would ever be justified. Nozick, however, distinguishes between carrying out an act of free will and the act of "flouting" the requirements of morality. To show that one has flouted a moral law it is only necessary to prove that one was aware of what he or she was doing. Nozick therefore claims that he has avoided the requirement of free will, because even if one's actions are determined, one could still be aware of having acted immorally. This solution of course does not resolve the problems about moral disagreement that we identified previously.

A separate retributivist approach to the challenge of determinism can be taken from what is often called the "pragmatist" tradition, which includes the work of Wittgenstein. According to this tradition, in answering philosophical questions, it is helpful to look at the way we actually speak when assessing whether one is responsible for a given action. Setting aside for the moment the question of whether the determinists are correct, let us focus solely on the language people use to describe responsibility. Most people speak as if individuals are responsible for their actions in certain situations and not responsible in others. While in the example of the forced stabbing, few people would claim the stabber was responsible, in many other instances they would say precisely that. Consider the case of Susan, who woke up in the morning and decided that she would buy a knife at the store and stab the first person she saw. Assume Susan was in good mental condition, had planned the act before the fact and carried it out. The following statements about Susan's act would be appropriate and I believe common: "Susan stabbed her victim. She intended to stab her victim. She is in good mental health. Therefore Susan was responsible for stabbing her victim."

Aside from the question of appropriate punishment, most people would speak as though Susan were responsible for the crime. A discussion of free will and determinism would not seem to be relevant to most people. In contrast, consider the following statement which would be quite odd in ordinary language: "Although Susan stabbed her victim, she was not responsible for doing so because she lacked free will, as do all people."

While responsibility might be an issue in a case in which someone was possibly insane, this concern does not arise when most people are discussing a case in which mental health is not an issue. Most people do not dwell on the issue of species-wide determinism in assessing individual responsibility. The pragmatist draws on the common vocabulary in addressing determinism. For the pragmatist, the larger question of whether or not determinism is valid is less important than the perspective of most people in evaluating action. Since most people speak as if it is possible to be responsible, perhaps that fact is more worthy of consideration than the determinist view that humans do not have free will.

At this point it might be sensible to ask the pragmatist, "Could most people not be mistaken in their manner of speaking?" In other words, perhaps people speak as if individuals have free will even when they really do not. Pragmatists respond, however, that our language determines our reality. When one goes to court, the terms "guilty" and "not guilty" determine a great deal about the future of a person on trial. The issue of whether these terms are ultimately based on a mistaken foundation is irrelevant to the fact that they are necessary to use. To return to our earlier example, while some people might be wrong in speaking about the earth as though it were flat, and it might be sensible to correct these people, it does not seem appropriate to claim that it is a mistake to speak in terms of guilt and responsibility. Rather, these terms seem essential to our basic way of life.

Those who do not accept the pragmatist response will be brought back to a debate over free will. If it turns out that determinism is valid, the larger question arises as to whether or not retributivism can rest on a form of responsibility separate from free will. As we will see, philosophers such as Frederick Nietzsche think the answer here is no. Before examining this claim, however, I would like to explore some other philosophical issues raised by retributivism.

The Assumption of Obligation

Retributivists also face a challenge from those who argue that one's particular circumstances in life often contribute to criminal acts. Without making the broader claims that determinists raise, these critics point out that it is often those who commit crimes who have been most abused by a given society, including abuse as children. This is especially the case when it comes to those who have committed capital crimes. Furthermore, those who commit the most serious crimes often grew up in poverty and/or live in poverty at the time their crime is committed.

It could be argued that abuse or poverty is responsible for these crimes. On this view, to hold the criminal responsible is to blame the victim. Perhaps society at large, rather than the individual who committed the crime, should be found responsible for criminal acts, although it would seem that the earlier views of rehabilitation and general deterrence, which do not rely on the assumption that individuals can be responsible for their crimes, offer more adequate support for this perspective. The retributivist, however, need not abandon the claim of responsibility to respond to this challenge. First, the retributivist can respond that the fact that some are not responsible for crimes does not imply that all are not. In fact, the retributivist argument only addresses one's responsibility in particular circumstances and leaves room for the claim that those who have not been abused by family or society are responsible for their crimes. The philosopher John Rawls, for example, has argued that one's responsibility in regard to the law increases proportionally to the degree that one is treated well in life. In his words, the top tier of society holds certain "obligations" not required of those who have not benefited as greatly from society.

In a practical sense, this view is incorporated into the legal decisions of judges who see poverty and abuse as mitigating circumstances in criminal cases. In other words, poverty or abuse could be seen to lessen the degree of responsibility for a crime. In extreme cases of abuse, perhaps no punishment is deserved. Consider, for instance, an extreme case in which an individual is seldom fed and is kept in a cage for his entire lifetime. Perhaps if such a person were to commit a crime, he could be judged not responsible and thus not be punished. Most people fall on a continuum between this extreme and no abuse, but there is no reason to think that their degree of responsibility cannot be judged accordingly. In incorporating these practices, the retributivist could consistently claim that punishment should be less extreme for poor, abused criminals than for wealthy criminals who have not been abused. This claim is consistent with Nozick's formula that appropriate retributive punishment should be determined by multiplying responsibility by the degree of seriousness of the crime.

Notes

1. I would like to thank Amy Gutmann for pointing out the importance of the distinction between "fit" and "desert" to me.
2. Van den Haag and J.P. Conrad, *The Death Penalty: A Debate* (New York: Plenum Publishing, 1983). Reprinted as *The Death Penalty: Opposing Viewpoints* (1997), p. 59.
3. Ibid., p. 61.
4. Contemporary philosophers have tended to be sceptical of the theory the way I have stated it. It is, however, widely held amongst anthropologists. There are many excellent introductions to the theory of moral relativism. In *Morality: An Introduction to Ethics* (New York: Harper Collins, 1972), Bernard Williams argues against "vulgar relativism" but later goes on to defend a more sophisticated relativist position. Also see J. Rachels, *The Elements of Moral Philosophy* (Philadelphia: Temple University Press, 1986).
5. See Nozick, *Philosophical Explanations* (Cambridge, MA: Harvard University Press, 1981).

7 Nietzsche's Critique: The Link Between Deterrence, Retribution and Revenge

Before I conclude Part I, we should examine the views of a thinker who challenges the entire method we have been proceeding with thus far. According to Frederick Nietzsche, both the retributivism and deterrence principles suffer from a common flaw: both theories are vengeance in disguise. In fact, as Nietzsche sees it, the attempt of both views to create a consistent basis for punishment and a justification for punishment actually produces more violence than would result if punishment were merely enacted when individuals felt violent urges. His claim rests on the insight that the acts of vengeance committed by individuals who have been wronged are not nearly as violent or harmful to society as is the havoc that the state causes through organized punishment.

Nietzsche distinguishes between those who affirm their desires and continually act spontaneously and those who repress their desires and act only based on reason. The former group he considers "noble" and healthy souls, while the latter group are "priests" for whom "everything becomes more dangerous, not only cures and remedies, but also arrogance." Among the "cures" that the priests wield is organized punishment, which in their hands becomes more vengeful and more dangerous than it would be in its original form. By priests, Nietzsche means not only clergy, but also all who attempt to provide moral justifications for punishment. According to Nietzsche, the nobles are characterized, in contrast to the priests, by their willingness to act spontaneously. If they feel anger towards an individual they simply act on their anger. As a result, Nietzsche claims, the nobles have no need for vengeance and seldom desire that their enemies be formally punished.

In contrast, the priests allow their hatred to fester. Rather than acting on their hatred, they repress it. The result is that all of this anger builds up over the long run and becomes more extreme. It is never released spontaneously, but is rationalized and eventually is expressed as formal punishment. The priests try to justify their own vengeance with a language of morality, which in turn only creates more violence. The pain of punishment is limited when it is in the pure form of anger, but once one attempts to legitimize this process it becomes the "most abysmal hatred."[1] The vengeful motives of the priests are masked and at the same time made worse by the fact that they speak in moral terms. Specifically, Nietzsche argues, vengeance is masked by the traditional retributivist terms of justice and responsibility: "Now I can really hear what they have been saying all along: We good men–we are the just–what they desire they call, not retaliation but the 'triumph of *justice*'; what they hate is not their enemy, no! they hate 'injustice,' they hate 'godlessness'" (original emphasis).[2]

Nietzsche argues that the priests' way of speaking intensifies the hatred motivating punishment and turns it into an ugly vengeance. As Nietzsche sees it, the real danger in the priestly form of vengeance is that it dominates our thinking about all issues, not just punishment. In effect, it has infected our consciousness. Our entire way of thinking makes us slaves to the priestly vengeance. This is nowhere more evident than in the feeling of responsibility and guilt that individuals feel when they have done something "wrong." While retributivists see guilt as an appropriate feeling when one has done something wrong and indeed justifies punishment, for Nietzsche it is merely a tool manufactured by those who seek vengeance and domination. Through a process which he labels "mnemotechnics," individuals have historically been made to feel guilty and responsible for their actions by those priests who solely want power. The priests use this guilt as a means to that power:

> This precisely is the long story of how responsibility originated. The task of breeding an animal with the right to make promises evidently embraces and presupposes as a preparatory task that one first makes men to a certain degree necessary, uniform, like among like, regular, and consequently calculable . . . in short, the man who has his independent, protracted will and the right to make promises–and in him a proud consciousness, quivering in every muscle, of what has at length been achieved and become flesh in him, a consciousness of his own power and freedom, a sensation of mankind come to completion . . . The proud awareness of the extraordinary privilege of responsibility, the consciousness of this rare freedom, this power over oneself and over fate, has in his case penetrated to the profoundest depths and become instinct, the dominating instinct. What will he call this dominating instinct, supposing he feels the need to give it a name? The answer is beyond doubt: this sovereign man calls it his conscience.[3]

The point here is that our feelings of responsibility, the very same feelings retributivists use to justify punishment, are no more than a tool that the powerful use to dominate its population. In contemporary times, this power rests with the state that punishes. The price of internalizing this feeling of responsibility is that we have lost any sense of individual freedom. In a sense, our collective conscience has made us into slaves.

Nietzsche's claims pose a challenge to both retributivists and advocates of deterrence. For the latter, Nietzsche's claim is that without modern punishment we would actually have less crime than we do now. In other words, modern punishment increases, rather than deters, crime. In response to the former, Nietzsche claims that individual responsibility, far from being a justification of punishment, is just a by-product of social power relations. Both these claims amount to the accusation that rather than offering theories of justice, both deterrence and retribution simply rationalize vengeance and power. In the following sections, I will evaluate the degree to which both of these theories are rooted in commonly invoked theories of justice and morality. If the justifications fail, the consequences are extreme. Nietzsche's critique might reveal that our practice of punishment is merely about power and not justice.

Before we go on to examine these justifications, I would like to examine two reasons why Nietzsche's theory is useful but not completely true. First, even if Nietzsche is correct about the vengeful roots of our current system of punishment, history cannot serve as an indictment of the present. Many institutions have been founded with ideologies that have later been discarded– think of secular schools with religious beginnings. Second, and perhaps more importantly, if Nietzsche's claim is correct, and justice merely serves to mask vengeance in our current system of punishment, this does not mean that reform towards a just system cannot take place using the tools of justice. Namely, a valid conception of just punishment could be used as a place from which to critique the current system. Some might object that it is foolish to claim that a term used in the past as an instrument of oppression can be used for reform. The model has worked before, however. Slavery, after all, was in place at the time the US constitution was enacted, despite the preamble's guarantee of equality–indeed, the moral language of equal protection was used at the time to justify the institution. The Constitution's guarantee of equality, however, has been used throughout American history to battle racism and segregation. The 1954 landmark case *Brown* vs. *Board of Education*,[4] which ended segregation in the South, was based on many of the same constitutional principles that had previously served to oppress African Americans.[5] As was true for equality, the abuse of justice does not taint all attempts to find a just system of punishment. Despite a past and perhaps a present abuse of the term to justify vengeful punishment, true justice is still within society's grasp. Nietzsche's challenge can be met with a just conception of punishment despite the fact that the claims of justice have served to oppress in the past and continue to do so.

Notes

1   F. Nietzsche, *On The Genealogy of Morals* (trans. N. Kaufman) (New York: Vintage Books, 1989), p. 34.
2   Ibid., p. 48.
3   Ibid., pp. 59–60.
4   *Brown* vs. *Board of Education* 1954, 347 US 483, 74 S. Ct 686, 98.
5   This point is best made by Ronald Dworkin in his *Law's Empire* (Cambridge, MA: Harvard University Press, 1986). Dworkin uses the analogy of a chain novel which begins with a basic principle and struggles until the conclusion to live up to this principle despite a series of conflicting events. Like the novel, Dworkin argues, American history began with very strong principles and the story of America is an attempt to live up to these principles.

8 From Punishment to Ethics and Political Justice

In previous chapters I have attempted to examine and analyze common approaches to the death penalty and punishment. In Chapter 1, we explored the problems with a debate about this issue which rests solely on appeals to the emotions of vengeance or pity. A system of punishment based on vengeance in particular, I argued, was flawed due to its indeterminate nature. A consistent system of reasons rather than emotion, I concluded, would be a more appropriate tool for determining punishment.

After analyzing the limitations of allowing emotions to determine our actions, I then moved on to examine various types of reasoning that could be applied to the issue. While problems accompanied both retribution and deterrence, the two approaches had the advantage of seeking a consistent single standard in determining punishment. There is, however, still a major dispute as to whether or not either system of reasoning justifies the death penalty. In Chapter 6, we came full circle and explored the connection between retribution and revenge. In Chapter 7, however, the entire project that I have been pursuing –the attempt to find a legitimate justification for punishment–was challenged by Nietzsche's theory of punishment. In the chapters to come, I will try to face Nietzsche's challenge: Are there any legitimate theories of punishment? If so, what moral basis do they have?

One method to be used when approaching these questions would be to go on to discuss whether particular theorists of punishment support capital punishment or abolition. Invoking deterrence, we could ask: Does the death penalty actually deter crime enough to justify the punishment? Invoking retribution, we could ask: Do murderers or rapists deserve the death penalty? Both questions assume a specific theory of punishment. As we shall see, many arguments both for and against the death penalty proceed in precisely this way: they take their theoretical assumptions for granted by simply examining the issue from within a specific framework. We will explore such approaches, especially as they are manifested in the Supreme Court's analysis of the death penalty issue at the end of Part I. In these cases, the Supreme Court Justices assume a specific theory of punishment. First, however, I believe it is necessary to inquire into which approach is justified in examining how we should punish. To do this it will be necessary to examine the philosophical roots of the approaches we have been examining. As we will see in the next few chapters, both deterrence and retribution have their basis in broader philosophical schools of thought in the area of political philosophy and ethics. In order to explore these principles for punishment, it is necessary to examine the larger theories from which they sprang.

There are significant ties between the specific question of why we punish and the fields of political philosophy and ethics. While punishment deals with the way we should act in a given circumstance–namely, when a crime has been committed–the field of political philosophy deals largely with finding a system of reasoning that is appropriate to political decision making. Since punishment is a subset of these decisions, it is necessary to explore this wider discussion. The jump to ethics is also appropriate. Ethicists ask what method we should use in making all decisions. While some ethicists have argued that their field should focus only on individual actions and not political actions, some political philosophies are actually rooted in ethical theories. In fact, the debate between those who favour deterrence and those who favour retribution in punishment can be linked to a much broader debate in ethical theory between those who claim only consequences are relevant in evaluating action and those who claim that intentions are the only relevant criteria. Those who favor deterrence in evaluating punishment can find justification for their beliefs in the former, whereas those who favor retribution find justification in the latter.

The histories of ethics and political philosophy are long, and there is not sufficient space in this book for a comprehensive review. Instead, I will focus on examining the theories that lie at the heart of most people's assumptions about punishment. First, I will show how these theories are rooted in two completely different conceptions of justice. From there I will demonstrate that these theories which are rooted in justice result in specific theories of punishment. Finally, I will demonstrate how these theories of punishment have influenced Supreme Court decisions on the death penalty.

As I will show, particular systems of ethics result in differing models of political decision making, which in turn lead to different conclusions about "just" punishments. First, we examine the approach to ethics which has become known as "utilitarianism." For utilitarians, the consequences of an action determine its rightness or wrongness. In politics, the "just" action is similarly dependent entirely on bringing about positive consequences. The same is true for just punishments. As we shall see, utilitarians offer a very specific criterion for measuring the merit of a given consequence.

In contrast, retributivists present a theory of punishment which completely ignores the consequences a given punishment has for society at large. As we have seen, for retributivists, punishment must be based entirely on what is deserved. This approach to punishment is rooted in a theory of ethics known as "deontology." I will focus on the roots of retributivism in the philosophy of Immanuel Kant, perhaps the most influential of deontologists. His ethical theory, I will show, provides a solid basis for retributivism.

9 Philosophical Foundations: Utilitarianism and Deterrence

While general deterrence, singular deterrence and rehabilitation all form distinct principles of punishment, all three share the common characteristic of justifying punishment in reference to its effect on society at large. The particular circumstances of a crime, guilt, and the degree of punishment, are all determined by this characteristic. This method of justifying punishment is rooted in the philosophical tradition known as "utilitarianism." For utilitarians, all questions of correct action can be answered by examining the consequences of each action. If utilitarians are successful in showing that all action, including political action, must be evaluated in reference to consequences, then it would seem to follow that punishment must be evaluated in the same way. In attempting to find a just punishment, they will argue, it is necessary to examine the overall effects that punishment would have on a given society. In exploring the validity of the utilitarian theory, I will begin by examining the work of Jeremy Bentham, the founder of utilitarianism.

For Bentham, all questions of justice are essentially questions of human psychology. He argues that the "right" is not an abstract concept but a principle that can always be reduced to human desire. Whatever pleases humanity as a whole is right, while that which displeases it is wrong. In Bentham's words, "mankind is under the governance of two sovereign masters, pain and pleasure."[1] Bentham's claim rests on the assumption that all people act in accordance with two rules: first, all people pursue pleasure; second, they try to avoid pain. If a theory of justice is to be sensible, it must be based on these two premises. Bentham's "principle of utility" states that decisions which "produce benefit, advantage, pleasure, good, or happiness" and "prevent mischief, pain, evil or unhappiness" are always the best to make.[2] All other attempts to develop a theory of justice, according to Bentham, will fail to take account of people's actual motivations and thus will not succeed.

Bentham's theory is dependent on the assumption that the amount of pleasure or pain that an individual feels over a period of time can be measured. He proposes a unit of measurement known as a "util." These units can be determined

51

through a combination of intensity and duration of pleasure. Ethical decisions–including all political decisions–should be based on whether or not the total number of utils present in all members of society would be maximized by a given policy. Consider the following example in which a choice must be made between a sausage and a pepperoni pizza. Suppose that a group of five people was given a pizza with sausage, to which three of the people had a reaction of 5 utils each, for a total of 15 utils. Suppose that same group was given pizza with pepperoni, and they each had a reaction of 4 utils, for a total of 20 utils. On Bentham's view, the principle of utility would demand that they choose the pizza with pepperoni.

As far as Bentham is concerned, all theories of justice which do not rest on the principle of utility are "nonsense." An example of this is the retributivist claim that punishment must be morally deserved. As we have seen, the retributivist defines desert by "what is moral" or "what is appropriate." This moralistic approach depends on an objective claim. For Bentham, however, morality, appropriateness–indeed the very ideas of justice or right and wrong –must be explained in terms of pleasure if they are to make any sense. Right must mean simply that which maximizes utility. Wrong must mean simply that which does not maximize utility.

When applied to punishment, the theory of utility provides a foundation for the theory of deterrence. According to Bentham, the act of punishment is nothing other than an imposition of pain. In his words, "punishment is an evil." It therefore can only be justified if it maximizes pleasure. In situations where punishment results in general and singular deterrence, this is often the case. Consider, for instance, the amount of pleasure that is created when a person who has been convicted of murder, and who would kill again, is detained in prison for a lifetime. The pain of a life lived in prison is enormous. However, when this degree of pain is measured against the entire life of pleasure that would be maintained among future victims of this individual, combined with the pleasure of the families of these future victims, utilitarians would argue that the murderer's pain is worth fewer utils. The principle of utility would seem to lend even more support to punishment in cases in which others would be deterred from committing crimes as a result of punishment. In these cases, the total amount of pleasure to be measured includes not only that of the potential victims of the person being punished but also the pleasure of the potential victims of those deterred. In addition, by deterring others from committing crimes, the society is saved from having to enact the pain of punishment on the potential criminals.

Bentham's theory of utility seems to provide a consistent criterion with which to judge both when to punish as well as how much to punish. Several of the same problems that we examined when looking at deterrence, however, arise with this theory. First, the theory could provide a justification for not punishing those who are guilty of committing a crime. Consider the case of an elderly person who commits one heinous crime just to experience a thrill. Imagine further that the person was no longer ambulatory and could be guaranteed never to do so again. What would prevent the state from releasing someone in such a situation? One might respond that even in cases in which singular deterrence is not necessary, punishment is needed on the grounds of general deterrence; crime might increase if the public knew certain crimes could be carried out without consequence. If, however, the state hid from the public the fact that the person was not punished, utility would not decrease. The state could, for instance, claim that no crime was actually committed. Criteria irrelevant to guilt could determine punishment under utilitarian policies.

In Chapter 4, "General Deterrence," we saw examples in which the fame or celebrity of an accused criminal, or the particular role he or she played in society, could influence the rate of general deterrence caused by his or her punishment. Utilitarianism leaves open even more of an opportunity for seemingly irrelevant factors to influence punishment. Remember the case of John, an extremely popular politician who was effective in bringing about pleasure in society in a manner that no other politician could. If John committed a crime, his constituents would be very unhappy, and society as a whole would suffer from his imprisonment. Even if he were guilty, the effect of punishing would be disastrous. On utilitarian grounds, it might be justified to release him. Utilitarians, therefore, run the risk of justifying the release of criminals.

Second, it seems that the theory could justify punishing innocents. While social utility is necessary for punishment, it is not clear that this necessity would require that those punished be guilty of a crime. Perhaps, under utilitarianism, unpopular people could be condemned if doing so promoted utility. Assuming the state presented the person as guilty, it would seem that in this case pleasure would be increased as a result of general deterrence by giving a population the satisfaction of seeing an unpopular person punished.

Third, the theory might allow for excessive punishment. If utility is the only criterion for judging the degree of punishment, in some cases punishing minor offences severely might create a lot of pleasure for a given society. For instance, if a crime was deeply offensive to individuals but not severe, a large degree of punishment might seem warranted. Flag burning, for instance, is deeply offensive to many veterans. While few would argue that the action deserves a lifetime in prison, at a time of nationalistic fervour, such a punishment might create enough pleasure in a given society to justify the penalty.

Fourth, the theory would result in inconsistent punishments. Since factors such as guilt and desert are replaced by pleasure in determining punishment, those who had committed similar crimes could be treated very differently. Guilt demands that only those who have committed crimes be punished while desert demands a consistent and moral system of determining the severity of punishments. Utility, however, fluctuates with changing circumstances, such as the time and place of the crime. It can also fluctuate based on personal characteristics. Utility, it could be argued, necessitates the abandonment of the principle that like crimes be treated alike. As a result of its inconsistency, many claim that utilitarianism is capricious: factors unrelated to the rightness or wrongness of the individual actions can play a huge role in determining punishment. Popularity, and the particular mood and temperament of a given population seem to be unjust criteria with which to judge an individual.

These four criticisms can be combined into a general critique of the utilitarian theory of punishment: the theory lacks respect for individuals. Bentham's method, the retributivist could argue, only recognizes the autonomy of separate people to the degree that it includes their own responses of pleasure and pain to political decision making. By lumping an individual's preference in with the mass, however, it seems all individuality is lost. After all, one person's amount of utils could easily be outweighed by mass sentiment. In trivial matters such as ordering a pizza, this might mean that one person's preferences are completely ignored. In a more serious matter such as punishment, it might mean that innocents are sacrificed and that severe punishment is inflicted on those who commit minor crimes.

Bentham acknowledges that his scheme of justice does not grant individual rights a primary role; rights must rest on the principle of utility. Despite this acknowledgement, however, he argues that utility will not result in the kinds of abuses described above. In fact, he argues that as a general principle, utility demands that a society adopt consistent principles in punishment. He explains, in a section entitled "Cases Unmet for Punishment" of his *Introduction to the Principles of Morals and Legislation*, that the second and third of the criticisms we introduced above can be answered by the principle of utility. First, he argues, a society can never punish the innocent. Bentham answers the concern about punishing innocents by claiming that it will never maximize utility to punish in cases "Where there has been no mischief."[3] His argument is not that it would be wrong to punish innocents, but rather that utility would not demand it. For instance, if people were aware that they could be punished for crimes they did not commit, a general anxiety might spread. This overall insecurity might in effect outweigh the particular benefits of punishing innocents on occasion. On average, Bentham argues, punishing innocents would result in less rather than more social utility. Bentham's point can be demonstrated by considering a society that occasionally did punish innocents in instances in which short-term social utility was maximized. If the people who lived in such a society found out about this practice, they would no doubt live with a certain amount of fear that they could one day be targeted for prosecution despite the fact that they did nothing wrong. The overall anxiety that would result from this knowledge over a period of time would most likely outweigh the occasional benefit that would come from punishing innocents. Furthermore, a general lack of faith in the justice system might develop among the populace. People might wonder, during all punishments, whether or not the government had targeted an innocent person. This lack of faith would also result in an overall decrease in social utility.

Second, Bentham rejects the notion that utilitarianism would result in excessive punishment. His principle demands that punishment only be inflicted to the degree that is absolutely necessary to maximize utility. Bentham argues that utility always demands less punishment when such a penalty is as effective as a large amount. Punishments beyond those which are necessary would only serve to decrease social utility. In his words, punishment must not be carried out "where it is needless, where the mischief may be prevented, or cease of itself, without it, that is, at a cheaper rate."[4] Therefore, according to this principle it would not be permissible to punish criminals with death if a lesser punishment–short-term imprisonment, for instance–could have the same effect.

An opponent of utilitarianism could object that these general principles only address what would most often be the case. Perhaps there would be exceptions to these rules. In these cases, breaking the rules would maximize utility. It might be true that on average it makes sense to act in the ways Bentham describes; the dangers lie in the exceptions. However, if people were aware that these principles were sometimes ignored, and innocents punished or the guilty punished excessively, the same general unhappiness could eventually pervade the society and therefore utility would be decreased rather than increased. To avoid even the perception that a society would violate these principles, utilitarians could argue, actions of this sort should never be taken.

These concerns have led some theorists to advocate a view that has come to be known as "rule utilitarianism," which can be distinguished from "act utilitarianism." Act utilitarians argue that decisions should be made so that utility is maximized in each individual circumstance. In contrast, rule utilitarians focus on developing a system of consistent rules, which a society needs to follow when making each decision. These rules are themselves justified by the fact that a consistent system would bring about the overall greatest utility. According to the rule utilitarian, even in specific instances in which breaking the rule would increase social utility, such action is not warranted. They argue that even though breaking rules might maximize utility in the short term, failure to abide strictly by these rules would in the long term lead to a state of insecurity among citizens and therefore decrease overall social utility.

Notes

1　J.S. Mill and J. Bentham, *Utilitarianism and Other Essays* (ed. A. Ryan) (London: Penguin, 1997), p. 65.
2　Ibid., p. 97.
3　Ibid., pp. 97–98.
4　Ibid., p. 102.

10 Hybrid Theory: Rawls's Act Utilitarianism

Rule utilitarianism is especially relevant when it comes to punishment. As we established in the previous chapter, it might seem justified on utilitarian grounds to sacrifice innocents, but doing so could undermine faith in the entire legal process and therefore lead to less utility. On the other hand, overall social utility might be maximized by a consistent system that occasionally failed to deter or maximize social utility in the context of a particular crime. The philosopher John Rawls has presented perhaps the best example of such a rule utilitarian-based system of punishment.[1] In his view, retributivism criteria are necessary in deciding if an individual should be punished in the first place. Retributivism is useful in "justifying a particular action" within the legal system. Utilitarianism, however, provides the justification for the entire system of punishment, including the use of retributivism in deciding who is punished in the first place. Retributivism is of use only because it results in long-term utility.

Rawls believes his hybrid theory satisfies our moral concerns with utilitarianism. The rules dictated by Rawls' hybrid utilitarianism necessitate that innocents can never be imprisoned and that guilt is a necessary condition for punishment. Rawls attempts to show that this thesis is based in our moral intuitions by positing a hypothetical conversation between a son and father. The son asks the father, "Why was J put in jail yesterday?"; the father answers, "Because he robbed the bank at B. He was duly tried and found guilty. That's why he was put in jail yesterday."[2] In asking about a specific case, the only justification for punishment is guilt. Rawls uses this intuition to justify the retributivist approaches in deciding if an individual should be punished at all.

If, however, the son asks for a general account of why we punish, the answer would have a different character. If the son asked: "Why do people put other people in jail?" Then the father might answer, "To protect good people from bad people."[3] This latter question, according to Rawls, asks for an overall justification of the system and here the former retributivist answer is inappropriate. Instead the system must be accounted for by a general utilitarian justification.

Rawls argues that his hybrid theory calls for judges, who deal with specific cases, to act as retributivists while legislators, who deal with the justification of the legal system as a whole, act as utilitarians. Despite the fact, however, that both systems are relevant to punishment, ultimately the power of the judges' retributive approach is dependent on the utilitarians' system of punishment. This is especially evident when it comes to deciding the length of punishment. As Rawls sees it, the amount of punishment should be dictated by the legislator's utilitarian concerns. Here Rawls reveals a potential weakness in his theory. Since Rawls bases the amount of punishment entirely on a utilitarian criterion, the theory does not seem to avoid the problem of excessive punishment. Since the degree of punishment is dependent on utilitarian criteria, it is not clear that there is anything to prevent excessive and erratic punishment when utility justifies it. While Rawls uses rule utilitarianism to prevent the possibility that innocents could be punished, he offers no such protection in regard to the amount of punishment that is justified.

Retributivists would most likely have another broader concern with Rawls's theory. They argue that a moral criterion is relevant in all matters of punishment. Although judges use retributivist language, in Rawls's view, this language does not ultimately justify punishment. These two problems are taken into account by the philosophical tradition, that gave birth to retributivism: deontology.

Notes

1   Rawls elaborates and defends this hybrid theory but indicates that he does not necessarily hold it himself.
2   J. Rawls, "Two Concepts of Rules," in J. Feinberg, *Philosophy of Law* (Belmont: Wadsworth, 1995), p. 652.
3   Ibid.

11 Philosophical Foundations: Retributivism and Kantian Deontology

For retributivists, two things are relevant in determining punishment. First, in determining whether or not an individual should be punished at all, guilt is the only relevant criterion. Second, in determining the amount of punishment, all that matters is what is morally deserved. Although retributivism is a well-developed theory of its own, it is rooted in a larger philosophical school of thought in moral philosophy known as "deontology." The two main tenets of retributivism can be understood and explored by briefly examining this larger current.

Deontologists argue that all moral actions must be judged without regard to the consequences of their actions. Perhaps the most famous argument for this view comes from the philosopher Kant.[1] According to Kant, moral theories that justify actions by their consequences disregard the dignity with which all humans deserve to be treated. In his terms, consequential theories, such as utilitarianism, result in individuals being treated as means to an end rather than as "ends in themselves." The following example illustrates Kant's point. A student finds a wallet and decides to return it to the rightful owner because she calculates that doing so will make her seem moral to her peers. The action would not be moral according to Kant because it was done for a purpose aside from the mere fact that it was the right thing to do. The student in this example treats the owner as a means to his or her own end of wanting to seem moral. For Kant, however, the only moral reason to return the wallet is that it has a rightful owner who deserves it back.

In addition to not using others as a means to an end, Kant argues that all moral action must be universally binding. If an action would fail to make sense as a universal law, it cannot be moral. He calls this duty to act as if each action were a universal the "categorical imperative." When Kant calls the categorical imperative the "universal law of morality" he means that it is never variable–even under extremely different circumstances, in different cultures or at different times. Kant's objection to views of morality that are based on consequences can be understood if we examine his claim that all moral actions must be universal. As we have seen, theories of punishment which are based on the consequence of deterrence will vary immensely depending on what circumstances surround the crime. For Kant, however, such a justification fails because it is not consistent and therefore cannot be willed as a universal law. In Kant's view, only principles that can be applied universally and consistently–even under very different circumstances–can 'command' or function as a universal law.

Now that we have briefly explored Kant's moral philosophy, we are in a position to explain why it serves as a basis for retributivism but not utilitarianism. In evaluating the ethics of punishment on Kantian grounds, two criteria would be relevant. First, we would ask whether the criminal is being used as a means to an end. Second, we would ask whether the state uses universal laws when punishing. As we have seen, under utilitarianism, the prisoner is used as a means for societal improvement. It thus fails the first part of Kant's test. Utilitarianism, as we have seen, also could demand different punishments for different crimes. It therefore also violates Kant's principle that moral actions must follow a fixed universal law.

Retributivism, on the other hand, abides by both of Kant's dictates. Guilt and desert are the only relevant criteria for retributivist punishment. Therefore, a person accused of a crime is being judged not as a means to other ends, but rather on the morality of his or her actions. As a result, punishment is not a violation of this person's dignity; it is deserved and therefore appropriate. In addition, since retributivist punishment must always be based on what is deserved, a universal standard is demanded by the theory. Retributivism does not use those persons accused of crimes as means to an end, and it is based on the notion that there is an objective and universal morality of punishment. As we have seen, retributivism has its roots in deontology.

I will argue in Chapter 12 that retributivism, partly as a result of its deontological roots, has led to one of the most famous anti-death penalty stances, that taken by Justice Brennan. On Kant's view, however, the retributivist theory of punishment necessitates the death penalty in cases of murder. Furthermore, on Kant's view, this penalty must be given out regardless of whether or not the penalty brings about any social benefits. For Kant, the death penalty is not only morally permissible, it is morally necessary in all cases in which it is deserved. In the following famous passage, Kant makes this point in harsh terms:

> Even if a civil society were to dissolve itself by common agreement of all its members (for example, if the people inhabiting an island decided to separate and disperse themselves around the world), the last murderer remaining in prison must

first be executed, so that everyone will duly receive what his actions are worth and so that the blood guilt thereof will not be fixed on the people because they failed to insist on carrying out the punishment.[2]

Kant's position here illustrates two reasons why a pure retributivist account of punishment has some limitations. Specifically, there are two problems with Kant's example. First, there is no benefit to executing the last murderer since there would be no society left to receive this benefit. Retributivist considerations might be necessary in avoiding the abuse of individuals for societal benefit when desert and guilt are used as minimum conditions for punishment. Here, however, they are the only criteria and justify seemingly pointless death. Second, Kant's emphasis is on relieving the "guilt" of the community rather than on what is deserved by the criminals in prison. This latter fact has led many commentators to suggest that revenge really is at the root of the retributive theory. Kant is explicitly concerned with the feelings of the community, not the morally correct action in response to crime. Among others, Nietzsche has suspected that the categorical imperative "smells of blood."

Despite Kant's harsh application of the retributivist theory to the death penalty question, the theory's emphasis on desert has led others to use it as a theory of restraint. Before I turn to one such modern application in Chapter 12, it is worth exploring the instances in which Kant himself argues that retributivism can recognize mitigating circumstances.

Kant argues that there are some instances in which the motivation that led one to commit a crime can be morally commendable or at least morally acceptable. Although in these instances crime itself might deserve death, praiseworthy motives deserve some mercy. Kant gives two such examples in *The Metaphysical Elements of Justice*. First, if an officer kills another officer in a duel in response to a challenge, the officer will be "risking his life" and will therefore "be able to demonstrate his military valor, on which the honor of his profession rests."[3] Since the officer acts with honor, Kant argues, he should not be executed even though he has broken the law by committing murder. Second, Kant argues that in cases in which a mother murders her illegitimate child, she should not receive the death penalty because she, like the officer, has acted with honor. Further, Kant argues, the mother should not be executed because she has killed a child who is not recognized by the law since it was conceived out of wedlock. The mother therefore does not bear as much moral blame as she would if she had killed a child that was the result of a "legitimate" marriage. In Kant's words, "A child born into the world outside marriage is outside the law ... and consequently it is also outside the protection of the law."[4]

Both of these examples allow for mitigation because of what Kant sees as morally worthy motivations. Despite his claim, however, these motivations are, from the contemporary point of view, morally questionable. Kant implies that one who refused to murder another when challenged would lack any honor. At the same time, he argues that the life of a child not born in accordance with a legal contract is worth less than one that is born within marriage. Both duelling and infanticide are not only illegal in contemporary times but are widely considered immoral. These examples, on some views, highlight a major problem with the retributive approach to punishment. They rely on moral judgements which seem to change with time and place. The Kantian claim to universal judgement, one might argue, is historically flawed, as is evidenced by his examples.

In addition to these instances of mitigation, Kant argues that in cases in which imposing the death penalty would result in massive social instability, the state should give a lesser punishment. Kant makes this pragmatic concession in the following passage:

> Anyone who is a murderer–that is, has committed a murder, commanded one or taken part in one–must suffer death . . . The number of accomplices in such a deed might, however, be so large that the state would soon approach the condition of having no more subjects if it were to rid itself of these criminals, and this would lead to its dissolution . . .[5]

This case is distinct from the earlier case in which a society that is about to disband must kill its last murderer. In that situation a society need not worry about the consequences to its stability because it will no longer exist after the murderers have been executed. Here, however, Kant is dealing with a situation in which giving the right penalty will produce instability in a society that does not wish to disband. Is Kant here admitting that retributivist theories must in extreme situations take utilitarian considerations into account? Does this in turn mean that Kant's is at root a hybrid theory? Although it appears that this is the case, closer inspection of Kant's position reveals that his reasoning remains purely retributivist. Kant's point is not that the criminal should be released because social utility will be maximized through greater deterrence. Rather, he is interested in preserving the existence of the retributive system of punishment. In effect, the survival of the system of punishing in the just manner depends on the occasional willingness not to do so. In these instances, retributivism is not trumped by utility but rather an individual instance of retributive justice is trumped by a concern for a retributive system of punishment.

So far we have discussed situations in which Kant believes retributivist theories call for restraint in giving the death penalty. In addition, Kant explains that retributivism calls for restraint in the way that criminals should be executed. Specifically, he argues "the death of the criminal must be kept entirely free of any maltreatment that would make an abomination of the humanity residing in the person suffering it."[6] Kant implies in this statement that some forms of the death penalty are so cruel as to deny the humanity of the person being executed. We can suppose that these include punishments that produce excessive pain or those which involve torture. While some forms of the punishment are excessive, however, Kant is clear that the penalty itself does not "make an abomination" of humanity. Still, Kant's notion that some forms of the death penalty are cruel and not deserved raises the question: is the penalty ever deserved in any situation? In Chapter 12, I argue that Brennan's approach to the death penalty is within the retributive tradition but offers a negative answer to this question. His strategy draws on Kant's last argument for restraint. Like Kant, Brennan argues that some punishments are so degrading that they deny the humanity of the criminal. While Kant does not include the death penalty in this category, as we will see in the next chapter, Brennan does.

Notes

1   The most concise and accessible statement of Kant's moral philosophy is his *Foundations of the Metaphysics of Morals* (New York: Macmillan, 1959).
2   I. Kant, *The Metaphysical Elements of Justice* (New York: Macmillan, 1965), p. 102.
3   Ibid., p. 107.
4   Ibid., p. 106.
5   Ibid., p. 104.
6   Ibid., p. 102.

12 *Furman* vs. *Georgia*

Thus far we have been concerned with an examination of punishment and the death penalty through the lens of debates in philosophy. However, here I want to explore a parallel between the philosophical approach to punishment and the manner in which those currently in power actually make decisions about punishment. Specifically, I will focus on the Supreme Court's approach to analyzing the constitutionality of the death penalty. In *Furman* vs. *Georgia*, 1972, the United States Supreme Court considered an appeal of three people who had been sentenced to death by separate juries in Georgia.[1] Before this case, the court had upheld state legislation which legalized the death penalty, but *Furman* ended this practice. In a groundbreaking decision, the majority of the court ruled that capital punishment was a violation of the United States Constitution. Specifically, the Justices concluded that the Eighth Amendment clause prohibiting "cruel and unusual punishment" rendered the death penalty unconstitutional. The decision was later overturned in 1976 in *Gregg* vs. *Georgia*.

The approaches taken by two Supreme Court Justices in *Furman* are rooted in the philosophical approaches we have been examining. Justice Brennan employs a retributivist attack on the death penalty, while Justice White attacks it from a utilitarian standpoint. The fact that the justices use differing philosophical foundations again demonstrates the point that a philosophical framework does not necessarily mandate a particular conclusion on a particular issue.

Before we proceed, it would be helpful to explore the connection between a philosophical discussion and constitutional law. Debates in philosophy are not limited by reference to one central text, while decisions in constitutional law are limited by the text of the Constitution. While *Furman* deals with the interpretation of the Eighth Amendment ban on "cruel and unusual punishment," I want to show in the following section that, at least in *Furman*, the methods of constitutional interpretation used by Justices Brennan and White were still dependent on their philosophical approaches.[2]

Brennan's Retributivist Anti-Death Penalty Stance

As we have seen, the theory of retributivism states that the appropriateness of a given punishment for a given crime is the only relevant criterion in determining the degree of proper punishment. Retributivists attack excessive punishments as undeserved. Indeed, according to Joel Feinberg, retributivism is a broad-tent theory encompassing all approaches to punishment that do not base their conclusions on the consequences of the punishment.[3] In *Furman*, Brennan's decision fits squarely in the retributivist tradition. It rests on the link between excessive punishment and human dignity. Simply put, punishments which are degrading to human dignity, he argues, are always too severe and thus never deserved: "a punishment by its severity should not be degrading to human dignity." Brennan believes the principle is an absolute which should apply to even the most brutal criminals.[4]

A primary example of a punishment which fails Brennan's dignity principle is the death penalty. "In comparison to all other punishments today," Brennan declares, "the deliberate extinguishment of human life by the State is uniquely degrading to human dignity."[5] Brennan's retributivist stance is revealed by his emphasis on the severity of the death penalty. By focusing on the excessive nature of death, Brennan attempts to show that it is never deserved.

Like any retributivist, Brennan faces the challenge of showing that the penalty is objectively too excessive and therefore never deserved. Punishments which are morally deserved, he claims, cannot involve the deliberate infliction of physical pain or extreme mental anguish. The death penalty, however, inflicts both physical and mental pain on those convicted of capital crimes. In the past, the court has found that punishments in which pain is knowingly inflicted are cruel and unusual. Among these, Brennan cites the case *Jackson* vs. *Bishop*, in which flogging was found unconstitutional precisely for this reason. As Brennan explains, the death penalty remained at the time the one government-sanctioned punishment in which pain was inflicted. Some proponents of the penalty might object that methods such as lethal injection have eliminated most of the pain from the act of execution. Brennan, however, rejects all such claims and argues "it appears there is no method available that guarantees an immediate and painless death."[6]

In addition to physical pain, the death penalty also inflicts mental anguish, according to Brennan. The emotional damage that is created from waiting on death row, he argues, is so extreme as to constitute torture. Many are driven to insanity as a result of knowing the exact time that their life will be extinguished. This phenomenon, as Brennan sees it, is clearly enough to demonstrate that the penalty violates the dignity principle and that the penalty is therefore excessive and not deserved.

The excessiveness of the death penalty is also evident in what Brennan describes as its "enormity." In the past, the court had ruled that expatriation was excessive because it "strips the citizen of his status in the national and international community."[7] Death, like expatriation, certainly takes away political identity, but it also does far more. While there is a possibility that the expatriate can regain rights in the future, death leaves no such possibility. In Brennan's words, it does away with the condemned's "right to have rights."

Like other retributivists, Brennan also faces the task of showing that an undeserved punishment, in this case death, can be distinguished from other deserved forms of punishment. In contrast to death, Brennan argues, life imprisonment can be deserved. Unlike death, life imprisonment does not violate either of the two criteria Brennan sets forth as a test of deserved punishment. First, no deliberate pain is inflicted on those in prison. While it is true that those in prison have in the past been tortured and ill treated, they have the right to seek redress in these matters. This brings us to Brennan's second point. The person imprisoned for life remains a part of the human family and retains the "right to have rights." A prisoner, for instance, retains the right to freedom of religion and freedom of speech. Those sentenced to death do not. In contrast to life in prison, death is cruel because it strips a human being of all rights and thus denies his dignity. On Brennan's account, a punishment which denied one's humanity and dignity to this extent could never be deserved by anyone, regardless of the crime he or she has committed.

Although the dignity principle is primary in determining punishment, Brennan does acknowledge that other criteria are also relevant. Among the other criteria he includes the necessity of the punishment, its arbitrariness and society's attitude toward the punishment. Why do these other criteria not dilute Brennan's retributivist stance? Brennan is clear that while other standards are relevant, the dignity principle reigns supreme. As he sees it, even if the death penalty did not violate these other provisions, he would still be tempted to find it unconstitutional: "I would not hesitate to hold, on that ground [the dignity principle] alone, that death is today a 'cruel and unusual' punishment, were it not that death is a punishment of longstanding usage and acceptance in this country."[8] Brennan recognizes that the historical support of the penalty demands that he offer additional arguments for its unconstitutionality. While he does appeal to other criteria, the dignity principle remains the central focus in determining whether or not a punishment is excessive.

Brennan's interpretation of the phrase "cruel and unusual" is thus dependent on a retributivist framework. His theory of punishment has a direct impact on his decision on the death penalty. Desert is given preeminence over other criteria. Ultimately, in Brennan's view, the penalty violates human dignity due to its infliction of physical pain and mental anguish, combined with its enormity. It is thus cruel and unusual and never deserved.

White's Utilitarian Anti-Death Penalty Stance

In contrast to Brennan's retributivist standpoint, Justice White takes a utilitarian perspective in his *Furman* decision. White's philosophical perspective is evident in his interpretation of the Eighth Amendment phrase "cruel and unusual." Like Brennan, White finds that the death penalty violates this provision of the Constitution. Unlike Brennan, however, White does not claim that the penalty is excessive by its very nature. Rather, he argues that the penalty is cruel because it is not effective in bringing about social utility. White assumes the utilitarian principle that individuals should be treated in a manner determined by how this treatment will impact society. In his words, he accepts the "morality and utility of punishing one person to influence another."[9]

In cases in which punishment is effective in deterring, it is justified. In the case of the death penalty, however, "the penalty is so infrequent that the threat of execution is too attenuated to be of substantial service to criminal justice."[10] In other words, due to its sporadic use, the death penalty is not an effective deterrent. Therefore, White concludes, it is cruel. White is very clear that this cruelty, however, is not an ahistorical characteristic of the penalty. Rather he argues that at the point in history at which the case was heard, 1972, the method of distributing the death penalty was cruel. Previously, "the penalty has not been considered cruel in the constitutional sense because it was justified by the ends it was deemed to serve. At the moment it ceases realistically to further these purposes." In other words, while in the past the penalty had a utilitarian benefit–perhaps because it deterred crime and was carried out more regularly, and therefore was not cruel–at the time of *Furman* it was ineffective and therefore violated the Eighth Amendment.

Like the utilitarian and deterrence views we examined previously, White's argument is based entirely on the effectiveness of the penalty at a given time. As a result, White's argument is not an absolute prohibition of the death penalty. If at some point the death penalty were used more and were effective in deterring crime, it would no longer be cruel and unconstitutional in White's view.

In fact, in a later death penalty case, *Gregg* vs. *Georgia*,[11] White argued that because the penalty would be used more frequently and more consistently, it would be effective in deterring crime and therefore was no longer cruel. The death penalty had only previously been cruel because it failed to serve a purpose. There was nothing in the punishment itself that made it cruel. Cruelty, in White's eyes, meant a lack of effectiveness. Once the penalty became effective, however, his objection was no longer valid. His utilitarian framework results in the reasoning that because more people would be executed, the penalty would become less cruel. Although it may seem at first glance that White reversed himself in these last two opinions, all three opinions are consistent on utilitarian grounds. In fact, he even leaves open the future possibility that the penalty could once again become cruel and unusual. If at some point the penalty once again fails to deter effectively, White would be forced to return to his position in *Furman*. While such fluctuation would be anathema to a retributivist, it is justified on utilitarian grounds.

Inequality and *Furman* vs. *Georgia*

A central issue raised in *Furman* and in the debate over the death penalty at large is the unequal application of the penalty. Specifically, opponents of the death penalty have argued that the race and class of defendants often influence the decision about who gets executed. Because these criteria should be irrelevant when deciding on punishment, they have argued, the penalty is given out unfairly and according to capricious criteria. How does the unequal use of a punishment affect the justness of a punishment? Specifically, how is equality related to the retributivist and utilitarian approaches of Brennan and White?

In constitutional law, this question has played a central role. In *Furman*, Justice Douglas, who wrote the lead majority decision, argued that the sporadic application of the death penalty was unconstitutional because it violated the Fourteenth Amendment guarantee of equal application of the law. Since the penalty was determined in a manner that left room for discrimination based on race and other factors, it violated this provision and was unconstitutional. Like Brennan and White, Douglas also argued the penalty was "cruel" and thus a violation of the Seventh Amendment. However, he linked cruelty to the provision regarding equality. In his view, unequal punishments are cruel. Douglas's argument does not seem to fit neatly into the retributivist or utilitarian categories, and his decision raises an important question for both theories: Can a punishment enforced unequally be justified on utilitarian or retributivist grounds?

In White's utilitarian decision, unequal application is a factor in arguing against the death penalty, but it is not a primary criterion; it is only relevant to the degree that it effects overall utility. White argues that the sporadic nature of the death penalty causes its ineffectiveness. It is thus the lack of utility resulting from its unequal application that makes the death penalty wrong. White assumes that if people are unsure that they will receive the penalty when they commit a crime, they will not account for the possibility of capital punishment when considering the consequences of their actions. While some have argued that equality is a morally necessary component in punishment, for White, like all utilitarians, equality is only relevant to the degree that it influences utility.

While inequality plays some role in utilitarian arguments, it is unclear that it is relevant to the retributivist argument. Pro-death penalty retributivists often find equality irrelevant to the justness of a punishment. According to van den Haag, equality of enforcement is irrelevant to the justice or injustice of a punishment. As he sees it, the fact that the penalty is sporadically enforced does not affect its rightness or wrongness. The only essential question is whether or not the penalty is deserved in a particular case. Van den Haag seems to be on strong retributivist ground here. The effect the penalty has on society at large and on other potential criminals is irrelevant to the two retributivist criteria for punishment: the accused person's guilt and the amount of punishment that individual deserves. For the retributivist, the wider societal context is often irrelevant to the question of whether a punishment in a particular case is deserved.

Like van den Haag, the anti-death penalty retributivist does not need to appeal to equality. Nonetheless, this is the approach taken by Justice Brennan. Although Brennan, as we saw earlier, argues against the penalty itself in *Furman*, he also deplores the unequal nature in which it is given out. But it is unclear why Brennan needs to follow this strategy. It is true that, on political grounds, Brennan might get more support for his stance by employing non-retributivist arguments, but these arguments are not a necessary part of the theory. In fact, it is possible that a concern with fairness in punishment could actually conflict with one of the main retributivist principles. The more frequent use of the death penalty might make it less discriminatory and, therefore, more fair. This use, however, would seem to violate the retributivist prohibition against using individuals as means to their ends; the end in this case would be the overall fairness of the policy.[12]

Brennan confirmed that his retributivist stance was not based on the objection that the penalty was not fair in cases subsequent to *Furman*. In *Gregg*, Brennan resisted the move of the rest of the court, which affirmed the constitutionality of the penalty. While both White and Douglas at times found the penalty was distributed more equally and less sporadically, Brennan continued to dissent in *Gregg* and other subsequent cases in which the penalty was found constitutional. Despite the appeal to equality that Brennan makes in *Furman*, equality is not a necessary component in his retributivist attack on capital punishment.

Furman Concluded

While both Brennan and White ruled that the death penalty was unconstitutional in the case of *Furman* vs. *Georgia*, their particular philosophies of just punishment resulted in very different approaches to dealing with this issue. Brennan is absolute and ahistorical in his criticism. For Brennan, the death penalty is *per se* degrading to human dignity and therefore too severe a punishment in any circumstance. White, however, leaves open the possibility that the penalty could become constitutional and later decides that it has. He is not opposed to the penalty itself, but merely doubted its effectiveness at the time he decided *Furman*. Here we have a major example of how one's philosophy of punishment can affect actual Supreme Court decision making about issues as fundamental as capital punishment.

Notes

1   408 US 238; 92 S. Ct 2726; 1972 US. Selections from the case are reprinted in J. Feinberg, *Philosophy of Law* (Belmont: Wadsworth, 1995).
2   By exploring these connections, I need not imply, although some certainly have, that there is no distinction between interpreting what the law is and arguing about what the law should be. Regardless of one's position on this debate it is evident that debates about proper punishment are relevant to the way the court has discussed the capital punishment issue.
3   Feinberg claims that retributivism and utilitarianism are mutually exhaustive. Those theories, which exclude utilitarian considerations, are retributivist. I need not make this claim to show Brennan is in this tradition. Rather I focus on his classic retributivist emphasis on guilt.
4   Although Brennan never makes reference to retributivism, his emphasis on this principle is enough to show that at least in the *Furman* decision he takes a retributivist and anti-utilitarian approach to punishment.
5   Feinberg, *Philosophy of Law*, p. 763.
6   Ibid., p. 764.
7   Ibid.
8   Ibid.
9   Ibid., p. 766.
10   Ibid.
11   *Gregg* vs. *Georgia*, 428 US 153; 96 S. Ct 2909.
12   I owe this point to Fatin Abbas.

13 The Link Between Retributive and Distributive Justice

Often, philosophical discussions of justice are divided into distributive justice and retributive justice. While retributive justice is concerned with punishment, distributive justice deals with how society should distribute its resources among its own population. As we conclude Part I, and make the transition to a discussion of welfare, it is reasonable to examine the debate over punishment in the context of broader philosophical concerns.

Some would argue that no discussion of punishment is sensible without reference to a wider discussion about the distribution of wealth in a given society. Marxists, for instance, often argue that retributive justice and the punishment it ordains merely exemplify the way the ruling class maintains its own power. In other words, in their view, punishment itself is a way of keeping the powerless from gaining power. Justifications of power are mere ideology. Thus the Marxist could argue that our entire discussion so far–with the possible exception of Nietzsche's critique–has been an exercise in helping to excuse the fact that oppressors in a given society keep the oppressed from rebelling. The Marxist claim seems to be borne out by statistical evidence. By far the majority of inmates in US prisons are from the lower classes. The bulk of this population, it could be argued, has been driven to commit crime by their material circumstances. Crime, in effect, could be interpreted as the bottom tier of our society simply trying to improve their circumstances. Punishment, the argument would go, merely serves to prevent this endeavor.

These claims serve as a useful way to examine the bulk of Part I. We have discussed punishment largely as an issue isolated from larger questions regarding the social dynamics of a given society: Why are the laws justified in the first place? What would constitute a just distribution of wealth?[1] Punishment is undeniably linked to these questions.

Consider, for instance, the consequences of punishment in a society in which the laws were completely unjust. In a society in which half the population were enslaved, punishment might never be justified. Slaves would be told that they are being punished for doing wrong when in effect the purpose of punishment would be to continue to keep them in bondage. The slave who refused to work a twenty-hour day and was whipped could have been told that he or she was punished for retributive reasons, that is, that he or she had done something immoral. Indeed, the Marxist claim that punishment serves only to enslave a given society would seem to be self-evident in this society.

There seems to be a distinction, however, between the role punishment plays in a slave society and in a society with a just distribution of wealth. If the law demands punishment in the context of justice, punishment would seem to be appropriate for those who break the law. In the context of a just society, the type of discussion we have had about why punishment is justified might be appropriate. In the context of slavery, the type of discussion we have had would seem to be mere propaganda put out by slave masters.

So where do we in the contemporary world stand? Are we speaking from the context of a just society and thus appropriately examining issues of retributive justice? Are we speaking from the context of slavery and thus issuing mere propaganda? Are we somewhere in between? In Part II, I attempt to examine these large issues. While at first welfare might seem disconnected from the issues we have dealt with in this chapter, it is intertwined with questions about distributive justice. By exploring these concepts I hope to examine whether or not the practice of punishment is ever itself justified.

So far, we have examined various explanations of why we should punish and exposed the strengths and weaknesses of each explanation. Now we will explore the broader theoretical context that frames both justifications and systems of punishment.

Note

1   I leave the enormous question of what would constitute such a distribution until Part II.

PART II
WELFARE, PROPERTY
AND DISTRIBUTIVE JUSTICE

14 Introduction to Part II: Is There a Right to Welfare?

Throughout Ronald Reagan's tenure as president of the United States, his speeches contained one recurring symbol–that of the "welfare queen." The welfare queen, according to Reagan and his supporters, lived a life of sloth, which was endlessly subsidized by the taxes of hardworking American families. Working families, in the Reaganite view, were entitled to tax relief to reward hard effort while those on welfare merely drained the country's resources.

Specifically, Reagan claimed that a significant amount of the money spent on the federal program Aid to Families With Dependent Children (AFDC) went to undeserving and lazy mothers. Part of Reagan's rhetoric was meant to draw attention to the supposed problem of fraudulent welfare claims by welfare recipients, but the image served a greater purpose. According to Reagan and many in the emerging Republican right, welfare encouraged an unhealthy dependency on government programs. All citizens who lacked inherited wealth or adequate financial support from family members belonged in the workforce, but the government discouraged them from working. These Republicans understood self-sufficiency to be one of the most important virtues, and government subsidies to poor people could only hinder their progress toward this goal. Implicit in these claims was the view that government should not provide a safety net or guarantee a minimum income.

Since the Reagan era, US public policy has continued to reflect the belief that there is no right to welfare. Currently, with the encouragement of the federal government, most states are moving toward a system in which welfare recipients are expected to work in government programs if they cannot find work in the private sector. In addition, many states have followed the Wisconsin model of limiting the amount of time people can receive welfare.

In the 1960s and early 1970s, the terms of the welfare debate could not have been more different. In 1972, the Democratic nominee for president, George McGovern, suggested a proposal that would seem radical to today's elected officials. McGovern proposed abolishing various state and federal welfare programs and replacing them with a nationally guaranteed minimum income for all Americans. Each family was to be assured to receive a salary with which he or she could secure the basic needs of life. Although President Richard Nixon objected that the McGovern proposal did not offer enough incentive for those on welfare to work, by mid-1972 his welfare proposal was virtually identical to McGovern's, according to *The New York Times*.[1] These proposals were buttressed by a widely held belief that all individuals had a right to basic welfare. Welfare, on this view, was not charity given by the government, but rather was an entitlement one should receive simply because one was a citizen or a human being.

While a debate over basic income dominated political discussion, around the same time period, lawyers and legal scholars were focused on whether or not there was a right to welfare embedded in the United States Constitution. In 1964, Charles Reich published the seminal article, "The New Property," in which he argued that under the due process clause such a right was guaranteed.[2] As Reich put it recently in reflecting on his original argument, "the function of property was to confer power on the individual." Since modern property relationships conferred this power to corporations rather than individuals, it was the government's responsibility, Reich argued, to relocate property in people's basic interests and needs. Thus the right to welfare should be secured by the state as a "new property."[3]

The debate over welfare has shifted greatly since then.[4] Nixon's and McGovern's position has been all but abandoned in contemporary US politics. While welfare has not been completely abolished, the nation has moved far from the notion that there is a guaranteed right to welfare.

To simplify the issue, we can distinguish three political positions in the welfare debate. First, call the defenders of welfare to work, who currently dominate the policy debate, "workfarists." Workfarists hold the assumption that there is no fundamental right to receive welfare payments. Someone only deserves an income when he or she participates in the economy by working. However, most workfarists agree that the government has at least some obligation to provide temporary work for those previously on welfare.

Second, call "welfarist" those who defend the view that all are entitled to a basic income regardless of whether they work. Workfarists and welfarists have different views on the value of work, but both suggest that the state has some obligation to provide for the well-being of its citizens.

Third, call the view that the government has no fundamental obligation to ensure basic welfare or workfare "libertarian." Libertarians think that provisions for the poor should only come from private charities. In their view, government's primary functions are to ensure a functioning free market and to protect citizens and their property. Any measures beyond this, including welfare payments, are not justified.

The three political views of welfare outlined above all differ on the basic question of whether all people have a fundamental right to welfare. For libertarians, the answer is a clear "no." For welfarists, the answer is clearly "yes." Workfarists lie somewhere in between. Although they believe that the government has some welfare obligations, they do not think that individuals have a right to welfare regardless of circumstances. In the following few chapters, we will move away from the terms of the contemporary political debate in order to explore the philosophical issues that divide the major political positions. Specifically, we will explore whether welfare rights have any strong philosophical foundations. Before starting, though, it will be helpful to be clear on what exactly the "right to welfare" means.

In particular, moral rights must be distinguished from political and legal rights. Moral rights exist as ethical guarantees with corresponding ethical duties regardless of contingent legal and political circumstances.[5] People should treat each other in accordance with their moral rights regardless of the institutions that support or do not support these rights. Even if it is agreed that all people have a moral right to welfare, it is unclear which institutions would be needed to secure this right. Libertarians, for instance, might recognize a moral right to welfare, but think that the corresponding duty to provide basic necessities should be met by private, not public institutions. An inquiry into the notion of moral rights, therefore, does not necessarily help to resolve our inquiry about the government's duty to provide welfare.

The right to welfare could also be understood as a claim about a constitutional right. Constitutional rights are generally defined as moral and political rights codifed into a higher law that cannot be repealed by a simple majority. Constitutional rights advocates see these rights as foundational to the just state. In some countries, such as South Africa, a fundamental right to welfare for children is explicitly ensured by the constitution. In the view of many, such a right is essential to a just state and must be guaranteed by the constitution. By contrast, most people do not interpret the United States Constitution as containing such a right. Libertarians would argue that there is not and should not be a constitutional right to welfare. Although welfarists and workfarists advocate government involvement in welfare, not all members of these groups argue for a constitutional right to welfare. Some welfarists argue that while welfare is essential it should not be written into a constitution. I will turn to the question of constitutional rights to welfare in Chapter 22.

The bulk of our inquiry in Part II will hinge on the third type of rights, political rights. If we are to discover whether citizens should have a political right to welfare, we must examine whether or not the state has a fundamental duty to provide welfare. Such a question is best addressed with a deep inquiry into the legitimate purposes of the state in the first place. What, we need to ask, makes for a just state? Are there any types of wealth distribution which are not legitimate in a state? Philosophically speaking, we must perform an inquiry into distributive justice. Such an inquiry will be fundamentally concerned with the justifications for different distributions of income and property. Like the earlier discussion of retributive justice, the question of distributive justice is concerned primarily with desert. On what grounds does someone deserve income of any kind? What types of income do various members of the population deserve? Must income be distributed equally? Is inequality justified when it benefits all members of society? Is it the state's role to protect income inequality, or rather to redistribute income in order to counter inequality? Only by answering these deeper philosophical questions can we begin to understand the roots of the political controversy over welfare.

In the following chapters I will examine the link between distributive justice and welfare within the context of major debates in the history of political philosophy. I will argue that those theorists who provide the strongest support for the notion that there is a right to welfare also argue for a major role for the state in redistributing wealth. It is true that one can be against redistribution but support some form of welfare.[6] I will show, however, that those thinkers who have been most hostile to redistribution, namely Locke and Nozick, have also been hostile to the notion that there is a right to welfare.

The history of distributive justice is too vast to consider in its entirety, so I will instead begin by considering the two most prominent approaches to welfare and distributive justice in the history of philosophy. These approaches vary in their answers to the welfare question because their justifications of state power vary. I focus on the major welfarist and anti-welfarist conceptions in the history of philosophy in the first half of this chapter. Specifically, I examine Locke's libertarianism versus Rousseau's welfarism. I then turn to the contemporary philosophical debate. Here I examine the various defenses of welfarism offered by Rawls, Walzer, Gutmann and Thompson versus Nozick's libertarianism.

Locke, I argue, offers a prime example of the libertarian approach to welfare, while Rousseau presents an exemplary welfarist attack on libertarianism. Locke understood self-ownership and private ownership of property to be the foundation of the state. This led him to argue that inequalities in property are just. Although Locke is often read to support the libertarian tradition, he does make some provisions for welfare and a version of workfare. I argue, however, that these welfare provisions are too minimal to make him a welfarist. They are best understood as a guarantee to private charity. Furthermore, his version of workfare, when examined closely, is close to a concept of punishment. Despite the seeming evidence to the contrary, Locke, I argue, is indeed a libertarian.

After elaborating on Locke's libertarianism, I examine Rousseau's attack on the Lockean notion of a natural right to property. Rousseau criticizes Locke for looking to the state of nature to determine justice. In rejecting the Lockean failure to secure welfare rights, Rousseau offers his own justification for a fundamental right to welfare. This right, he argues, is necessitated by the social contract, which does not demand pure equality of wealth, but which does demand an egalitarian distribution.

I move on to examine contemporary approaches to the welfare and distributive justice question. I elaborate the welfarist approaches of Rawls, Guttmann, Thompson and Walzer. I then go on to examine how Robert Nozick's libertarian approach challenges contemporary welfarism. Rawls, I argue, further clarifies and defends Rousseau's welfarist approach. Furthermore, Rawls' theory of justice provides a detailed justification for a strong state role in welfare. Specifically, I focus on how his contractarian device, the veil of ignorance, provides a defense for the right to welfare.

While Rawls perhaps draws most heavily from Rousseau's welfarist approach, his is not the only contemporary philosophical defense of the right to welfare. Michael Walzer also makes the notion of welfare central to his conception of justice, while at the same time critiquing Rawls's reasoning. In Walzer's view, welfare rights are justified by needs. Although Walzer defends certain kinds of welfare rights, he does not argue that redistribution of wealth should be the central concern of the just society. Walzer thus provides a welfarist alternative to Rawls.

I explore both libertarian and welfarist alternatives to Rawls by briefly examining what in the philosophical literature is widely labelled "the free-rider problem:" what should be done with those who are capable of contributing to a society but choose not to? Those who find the free-rider problem addressed in an unsatisfying manner by welfarists might be more sympathetic to a workfarist conception. I briefly explore the suggestion of Dennis Thompson and Amy Gutmann that a position of "fair workfare" is most justified. Their account of reciprocity leads to a notion of welfare tied to work but, I argue, remains welfarist.

While most of the discussion until this point will focus on the controversy over whether or not there is a political right to welfare, I devote the next section to exploring whether such a right, if it indeed exists, should be ensured as a constitutional right.

I will finally turn to a theory which challenges the basic notion that the concept of justice could be helpful in examining political issues. Karl Marx's ideology does not fit either within welfarism or libertarianism, but rather is useful as a criticism of the very idea of distributive justice. According to Marx, any attempt to establish a right to welfare must be doomed to failure, since rights are inherently libertarian and thus cannot secure an egalitarian material condition. He thereby fulfils the role Nietzsche played in Part I's discussion on punishment: he criticizes the very terms of the debate.

Notes

1   For more details on the McGovern proposal see G. Weil, *The Long Shot: George McGovern Runs for President* (New York: Norton, 1973). Nixon's proposal was profiled in *The U.S. News and World Report Guide to the '72 Election.* Both the Nixon and McGovern proposals fluctuated throughout the election. At one point McGovern wanted to guarantee an income of $4,000 to each family. After much criticism, however, he changed the figure to $1,000. Nixon had campaigned for a work requirement in order to receive welfare in 1968, but in 1972, supported incentives to move people from welfare to work, which did not resemble the time restrictions that have come with recent welfare reform proposals.

2   See C. Reich, "The New Property," *Yale Law Journal*, 1964, No. 73, p. 733. Reich has restated his position and added an ecological theme in "Beyond the New Property: An Ecological View of Due Process," *Brooklyn Law Review*, Summer 1990, Number 56, p. 731.

3   Although welfare-rights theorists like Reich were emboldened by the Supreme Court's decision in *Goldberg* vs. *Kelley*, 397 US 254 (1970). The court ruled that economic protection of the individual was a goal that needed to be balanced with other social goals which could have a higher priority. Despite the optimism of these theorists the court made it clear in later decisions such as *Mathews* vs. *Eldridge*, 424 US 319 (1976) that there was no constitutional right to receive welfare benefits. The court decided in that case that an evidentiary hearing was not required prior to the termination of disability benefits.

4   Some prominent political philosophers continue to hold this view. See P. Van Parijis, "Why Surfers Should Be Fed: The Liberal Case for an Unconditional Basic Income," *Philosophy and Public Affairs*, 20 (Spring 1991). I discuss other philosophers who also hold this view in later sections. Prominent among them is John Rawls.

5   See J. Thompson, "A Defense of Abortion," *Philosophy and Public Affairs*, 1 (Fall 1971), for an argument based solely on moral rights.

6   George Kateb is an example of such a thinker. See his *The Inner Ocean* (New York: Cornell University Press, 1994).

15 Locke on Property, Distributive Justice and Welfare

Defenders of the libertarian position have often turned to the writings of John Locke.[1] On the libertarian reading, Locke's view of justice is incompatible with the notion that there is a fundamental right to welfare. Specifically, they argue that Locke's view that the protection of private property is the central role of the state leads him to reject the notion that the state needs to ensure subsistence for all members of society. In this section, I will defend the libertarian reading of Locke and argue that while some commentators have pointed to some passages that indicate Locke believed in state welfare entitlement, he in fact does not. Libertarians are correct to argue that the right to welfare or any form of state-guaranteed welfare is not part of Locke's conception of distributive justice. In fact, Locke's views of private property do offer theoretical grounding to those who argue against any fundamental right to welfare. Indeed, historically welfarists like Rousseau have felt the need to undermine Locke's views over any others. While Locke offers no political right to receive welfare from the state, I demonstrate that Locke does claim individuals have a "moral right" to subsistence. This right, however, is a right to charity, not a political right.

Locke's view of distributive justice, and in turn his position on welfare, rests on the crucial claim that private property is guaranteed by natural law. Prior to the establishment of the state, Locke argues, individuals acquire and own property. Furthermore, individuals combine to form a state only to protect the property they acquire and own. Justice, then, requires the protection of private property and prohibits any massive wealth redistribution. Before examining why Locke's theory is hostile to redistribution of wealth and welfarist conceptions of the state, it is necessary to explore why he argues that private property is the fundamental basis of the state.

Locke's individualism and defense of private property are closely linked with his notion of "self-ownership." Locke begins with the premise that all people "own" themselves. As he puts it, "every man has a property in his own person."[2] As a result of the fact that individuals own themselves, Locke argues, they also own the products of their labor. When one produces goods as a result of working, she owns these goods in the same way that she owns herself.

This premise is as true in a state of nature (that is, the absence of any government) as it is in the most highly civilized society. As a result, individuals always possess a fundamental right to protect their own lives and to be free from the trespasses of others; that is, a Lockean individual is "bound to preserve himself." Furthermore, these individuals will reason that their own right to self-protection implies that others have the same right. According to Locke, individuals understand that everyone is bound not to "take away or impair the life, or what tends to the preservation of the life, the liberty, health, limb or goods of another."[3] Locke's view of self-ownership therefore results in what Isaiah Berlin calls "negative freedom," freedom consisting of the absence of interference from others. Humans in nature and in society are protected by rights and in turn recognize that they must not violate the rights of others.

Although people interact in Locke's state of nature, personal identity primarily springs from the individual, not from the individual's interactions with the surrounding community. Individuals become aware of the natural right to property by examining their "own hearts." The natural law of property and protection are not developed through social interaction or for social benefit. Rather they are embedded in nature and learned by individuals. On Locke's view, God has written the natural law, but individuals need not know God to have access to the natural law–they need only use reason to look within themselves.

Locke's individualism is further developed in his view of labor and property. In nature, since one's labor is merely an extension of one's body, the individual also owns the benefits ensuing from one's work. In fact, Locke argues that all the results of that labor actually become part of the person. We own our property in the same way we own ourselves. For example, if one toils on a piece of unoccupied land to grow corn and eventually makes that land productive, the corn, at least in a figurative sense, becomes a part of one's own person. In addition, Locke argues that by working, one can lay claim to the raw materials of nature with which one has toiled. Therefore, to return to our example, one cannot only lay claim to the corn but to the land one has made productive. In Locke's words, an individual "that mixed his labour with a piece of barren land . . . joined to it something that is his own." In doing so he or she "makes it his property."[4] Owning material goods is therefore as fundamental as owning one's self. In fact, Locke is content to claim that property itself is the most fundamental right. Since one owns oneself, the right to life is analogous to the right to property. Locke makes this point clear when he argues that while there are natural rights to life, liberty and property, all three can be subsumed under the general title of property.

Locke's account justifies major inequalities in wealth for three reasons. First, Locke argues that since some individuals work harder than others do, they are justly rewarded with more material goods. Second, some individuals have more talent than others. According to Locke, "merit may place others above the common level," and those so placed clearly deserve more goods.[5] Third, although Locke does not mention it, luck obviously plays a role in how much property one can acquire. In essentially agrarian communities, those born with an intelligence that allowed them to develop techniques that resulted in more crops might have to work fewer hours than those who did not. In addition, luck determines which members of society gain inherited wealth and which are blessed with weather faborable to their crops. Work is therefore fundamental for Locke. The amount of one's material goods should vary depending on one's talent and the effort with which he uses that talent. It will also vary due to one's luck.

Although Locke argues that all should abide by the same rules for obtaining property, he theorizes that opportunities for land acquisition, at least, were more abundant in the past than in more modern times. According to Locke, originally God gave all land to humankind in common. At the beginning of world history, there were therefore a great number of places to choose from as one decided where to work. As time went on, this land became divided up, and large pieces of formerly common land became privately owned. This fact did not pose much of a problem for Locke. In his time, he argued, there were still vast amounts of common land that could be claimed by motivated individuals. For instance, he claimed that America was one place where a great deal of land, more than in his entire home country of England, was available for acquisition.

According to Locke, despite the general availability of land, the possibility of transferring wealth (especially to one's descendants) magnified inequalities in wealth. What were originally minor inequalities due to unequal talent or effort in working could soon develop into more major ones.

In his *Second Treatise on Government*, Locke argues that the right to have one's self free from harm is fundamental. Equally fundamental for him is the right to transfer the wealth one has acquired to one's heirs. Ownership, in Locke's view, means that property owners can use their goods in the manner that they see fit. If they so choose they can give it to friends, transfer it to charity, or if they wish, leave it to their children. To impose limits on what one could do with one's property, for Locke, would be an unacceptable restriction of human freedom.

While limits on what one could do with one's property are almost non-existent in Locke's system, there are, however, some limitations on what one can do with one's own body. In order to understand these limits, it is necessary to explore Locke's notion of the natural law in further depth. In his view, the natural law guarantees all individuals a right to life, liberty and property. Part of the right to life, however, includes certain duties on the part of all individuals to preserve themselves; for example, one cannot sell herself into slavery or commit suicide. People who did either of these things would no longer have a life to preserve, and thus their natural rights would be worthless. In addition, these limits can be defended in terms of liberty. People who end their own lives limit their future freedom. They in effect end their ability to be free. Therefore, although individuals own themselves, there are some limits to that ownership. People cannot terminate their ability to have rights. In Locke's words, these rights are "inalienable."

The State as a Guardian of Property

We have explored why Locke believes that the right to property exists in the natural state and is ensured by natural law. He further argues that this natural right cannot be secured without the aid of the state. Without a great power to appeal to, an individual whose rights have been violated must himself punish the offender. However, as we have discovered, this process of punishment can only result in war, since emotion and revenge will replace punishment. The existence of law in nature, then, is not enough to prevent the collapse of the natural state. In order to reinstitute order and protect natural law, Locke posits that individuals accept a social contract and thereby establish the state. This consent is not explicit, according to Locke. Rather it is "tacitly" or silently implied by one's decision to live in a given community. This contract is a very limited one, since it exists only to effectively enforce natural law. Citizens surrender their right to retaliate and punish transgressors of the natural law, but only because they realize that the state can do a better job in punishing. In forming a compact, citizens are far from relinquishing any right to property. Instead, the transition is made from nature only to better secure this natural right. In other words, government recognizes this right of property, but does not create it. Locke also believes the state can protect the rights to life and liberty together with possessions better than individuals can in nature. Since we own property in the same way that we own ourselves, the notion that there is a right to property includes the rights to liberty and life. In my discussion of property throughout the rest of this chapter I mean, as Locke does, to include liberty and life as types of property.

For Locke, then, the state has a very specific function: to enforce consistent and clear natural property laws better than individuals acting alone. Since this is the only reason the state comes into existence, the state is legitimate only when it enforces these natural laws. Basing punishment on any criteria other than natural law, or claiming and redistributing the property of its citizens delegitimizes the state. Such actions amount to violations of the natural law by the state, and are conceptually no different from robbery. In Locke's words, any state which violates individual property rights puts itself in a "state of war" with the population.

From this description of property and the role of the state, it should be evident why theorists who want to argue against an entitlement or a right to welfare have turned to Locke. In Locke's view, property is fundamental. Far from having the right to redistribute wealth, the state's role is merely to protect private property. It is true that even for libertarians the state must take some property in the form of taxes in order to pay for the services necessary to protect property. A police service is needed to arrest those who trespass. Courts are needed to ensure that punishment is carried out fairly in contrast to the system in the state of nature. Fire departments are needed to ensure against damage. Still these taxes are only necessary to the extent that they better secure natural law. Anything beyond this, on the libertarian reading, is not only unjustified but also risks putting the state into a state of war with its citizens. A state which attempted to redistribute wealth would in effect be no different from a thief.

Locke's notion of distributive justice therefore allows for, and indeed ensures, the protection of unequal property relations. This inequality is guaranteed by natural law. The state is prohibited from redistributing wealth, and should any state engage in such action, it would lose its legitimacy.

Locke and Welfare

Despite the strength of the libertarian reading of Locke, some commentators seek to demonstrate that Locke had at least a minimal commitment to provisions for the poor. In their view, this commitment demonstrates that Locke demands the state engage in ensuring basic welfare for all citizens. Although their insights have helped to demonstrate that Locke cannot be entirely appropriated by libertarians, I argue that two aspects of Locke's philosophy suggests that welfarists are wrong to appropriate his writings for their cause. First, while he claims that charity includes a moral obligation on the part of those with wealth to give to the poor, he is clear that justice does not. As the state's function is to ensure justice, government does not guarantee maintenance of the poor. Second, the provisions of Locke's charity are too minimal for him to claim a right to welfare. Locke's comments about charity, I will argue, are tangential to a general theory which is based on private property and generally hostile to both the concept of redistribution and a state role in securing welfare.

A major objection to the concept of distributive justice outlined above focuses on its lack of guarantees for those who do not successfully compete. Some might lack the talent, luck, or even ambition to acquire any property at all. Does Locke's scheme of distributive justice allow for starvation? Is any guarantee offered against destitution?

In his discussion of the state of nature, Locke states that such problems are avoidable without the promise of state aid for two reasons. First, the land offers abundant resources, which far surpass humanity's needs. Second, since God gave humans property in order to survive, each person is only entitled to use as much land as he "could make use of."[6] Any wasted or spoiled property was to be forfeited back to the common: "The same rule of propriety that every man should have as much as he could make use of, would hold still in the world to suffice double the inhabitancy."[7] Later he explains his claim that the amount of property one is entitled to take is limited: "Though men had a right to appropriate, by their labor each one of himself, as much of the things of nature as he could use: yet this could not be much, nor to the prejudice of others, where the same plenty was still left to those who would use the same industry."[8] Because individuals are limited to "enough and as good" and cannot waste property, Locke believes scarcity will not arise.

Locke's proviso, however, stops short of guaranteeing welfare. The claim only creates opportunity for those who have "industry;" that is, in order to subsist, the poor individual must be able to work the land left over. Locke argued that in his own time, while land in England had largely been claimed, vast quantities of unclaimed and unowned property still existed abroad. This was especially the case, he argued, in America.[9] Far from offering an account of welfare at all in the form of a transfer payment, Locke offers the poor an opportunity for labour. No guarantee exists for those who cannot work due to disabilities or perhaps their extreme youth. Locke's proviso is therefore quite different from modern "workfare" laws, which often exempt certain classes of people from work.[10] The opportunity to work that Locke's proviso guarantees is not of much use to those who lack the ability to take advantage of it.

In response to my libertarian reading of Locke, someone who wanted to defend the view that Locke has a commitment to some form of welfare might claim that the above proviso serves as a crude model of a workfare provision that could be better implemented once the state is established. The proviso, they might claim, could serve as a right to work. This is clearly, however, not Locke's view. Far from enhancing the ostensible right to work established by the proviso, Locke argues that the establishment of a monetary system invalidates this right and it cannot therefore be a model. The proviso, as we have seen, is based on the notion that no goods should be allowed to spoil. Hoarded crops, for instance, would likely go bad and therefore should belong to all. However, according to Locke, once money is introduced into society, this spoilage provision is no longer relevant because value can be stored as gold or money, which cannot go bad. In Locke's words the proviso is nullified as a result of "the use of money, some lasting thing that men might keep without spoiling, and that by mutual consent men would take in exchange for the truly useful, but perishable supports of life." Gold and silver "may be hoarded up without injury to any one; these metals not spoiling or decaying in the hands of the possessor."[11] It is clear in Locke's account that the proviso only is binding in nature and is not applicable in the state.

One thinker has argued that the spoilage proviso does have a limited application in a society that has money.[12] While gold and silver cannot go bad, food itself can still spoil. Imagine a situation in which a speculator has purchased a barn full of bread. Furthermore, imagine that for some reason he has failed to sell the bread before its spoilage date. While the money the speculator used to buy the bread has not spoiled, it seems that the bread itself has. One might argue that the poor have the right to this bread. While this might be true post-spoilage, at the pre-spoilage stage, the speculator is arguably still making use of his commodity; he is waiting to have an opportunity to sell it. The spoilage proviso therefore is only helpful after the bread has spoiled. At this point it no longer has any use. The provision therefore falls short of allowing for any state-guaranteed welfare.

Although Locke offers no welfare guarantee, he does think his account of property will ensure against poverty for the most part. In his account, private ownership and the establishment of money will create even more abundance than that offered by nature. Hoarding money does not injure others in the same way that hoarding perishables does, but rather, as Stephen Holmes points out, the market that results from capital accumulation will make more goods available to all. The question remains, however: what will happen to those who have no money to buy even cheap products? It seems that the poor have no guarantee of being able to secure their subsistence in Locke's scheme when the market fails to distribute resources.

Stephen Holmes attempts to save Locke from a libertarian reading by pointing to a second Lockean proviso. Holmes argues that Locke provides the groundwork for state welfare payments in his *First Treatise on Government*. Holmes quotes Locke:

> We know God hath not left one Man so to the Mercy of another, that he may starve him if he please: God the Lord and Father of all, has given no one of his Children such a Property, in his peculiar portion of the things of the world, but that he has given his needy Brother a Right to the Surplusage of his Goods; so that it cannot justly be denied him, when his pressing Wants call for it. And therefore no man could ever have a just Power over the Life of another, by Right of property in Land

or Possessions; since 'twould always be a Sin in any Man of Estate, to let his bother perish for want of affording him Relief out of his Plenty. As Justice gives every Man a Title to the product of his honest Industry, and the fair Acquisitions of his Ancestors descended to him; so Charity gives every man a Title to so much of another's Plenty, as will keep him from extreme want, where he has no means to subsist otherwise.[13]

The above passage does raise questions about whether or not Locke believed in a right to welfare. The claim that the starving person has "a Right to the Surplusage of" the goods of the wealthy seems to indicate that Locke would favour some welfare. However, Holmes goes too far in claiming that Locke offers a "universal entitlement to welfare." Holmes is right to assume that the "Right to the Surplusage" implies a duty on the part of those who hold surplus wealth to provide for such a right. However, is this right and the corresponding duty moral or political? Is it the responsibility of government or wealthy individuals? Although Locke clearly feels the rich may have certain moral obligations to the poor, he does not necessarily believe that the state may legitimately enforce those obligations. Moral rights are not necessarily political rights. Locke seems, in fact, to indicate that the responsibility for upholding the "right to surplusage" is the individual's and that he is talking about moral, not political, rights. He claims it is a sin on the part of the individual wealthy "Man of Estate" to let "his brother perish," not that this is a sin of the community or state. Thus, although "Charity" may require the individual to donate to the needy, justice does not require the state to do so. In fact, Locke explicitly distinguishes between the "Title" given by "Charity" and the one given by "Justice." The latter requires work, and only work, to be rewarded by material goods, while the former is linked to individual duty. We see, then, that the passage Holmes cites is actually consistent with the libertarian reading. Property protection, not redistribution, is the role of the state, despite any inequality that might result.

Even this obligation of charity is quite limited for Locke, for it ensures against "extreme want" but does not ensure an income sufficient for a dignified existence. The implication is that if individuals could be brought to the level of poverty but not extreme poverty, then the obligations of the rich will have been met. Leaving individuals "wanting" falls short of the decent standard of living for which welfarists argue.

At the start of the section on property in the *Second Treatise*, Locke does claim that there is a natural right to "meat and drink." The statement, however, does not support the claim that there is an entitlement to welfare, as Holmes argues. At first glance, the phrase seems to indicate that the state (an enforcer of natural law) must ensure food for all. However, under my reading of Locke, the right to "meat and drink" in regard to the state is better understood as the right to obtain these products through work. It is a negative right not to be interfered with in the process of obtaining these products, rather than a positive entitlement to the products themselves. Reading Locke in this manner does not exclude a duty to charity or the ability to condemn the rich who allow the poor to starve. At the same time, the right implies the moral duty of the rich to provide for the poor.

Although Holmes alerts us to Locke's recognition of the need to address the welfare question, it is clear that Locke's view of welfare does not guarantee a political right to subsistence above the level of starvation. Instead he gives an account of a moral right to receive charity.

Locke on Charity and a Policy of Forced Work

So far we have used Locke's theoretical work to deduce his views on welfare. In real politics, however, Locke made his views on this topic quite explicit. In the testimony from 1697 published as "Draft Of A Representation Containing A Scheme Of Methods for the Employment of the Poor," Locke reveals that he believes that the state has no responsibility to provide "meat and drink" directly.[14] Instead, he argues, in most cases, the state's responsibility is only to coerce into work, violently if need be, those who can work. Provisions for those who are not able to work are few and far between, the amount of relief is minimal, and private citizens (not the state) bear responsibility for this relief. In the following few pages, first I examine the evidence of this text, and then I argue that Locke's notion of forced labour is not properly understood as relief at all, but as punishment for a potential violation of the right to property.

We have already noted Locke's claims that one's right to property is limited in nature. "Spoilage" is disallowed, and "enough and as good" must be left in common to allow others to prosper. Although the use of money nullifies this proviso, Locke is clear in his testimony that the economy provides "enough and as good" for the poor. Poverty exists, not because of a lack of opportunity to work, but because of laziness. "The growth of the poor" is the result of "nothing else but the relaxation of discipline and corruption of manners: virtue and industry being as constant companions on the one side as vice and idleness are on the other."[15] Simply put, if individuals all worked hard, poverty would be almost entirely solved.

Since work is in effect close to a cure-all, Locke must assume that most of the poor are capable of working. He does, however, recognize that not everyone has the same capacity for work. He divides the poor into three groups. First, there are those who can contribute nothing at all towards their support. Second, there are those who cannot fully support themselves, but are able to contribute partially to their own livelihood. Third, there are those who are able to maintain themselves by their own labor. Groups two and three are the most prevalent amongst the poor. As we shall see, this includes the handicapped and children as young as three years old. The first group Locke believes to be a small minority, and charity towards them is expected by the state, but, I will argue, is in no way ensured or mandated. While the expectation of charity seems to offer another place for those who resist the libertarian reading of Locke to point to, upon close examination it does not support a welfarist reading of Locke. Locke's focus throughout the text is on the majority of the two other groups of poor people who can and should be made to work.

Since in his view poverty primarily results from a lack of hard work, Locke argues that the state must force many of the poor to labor. The able-bodied poor who wander from their home "parish" should be targeted for forced labor. If found begging outside their home parish, the poor should be sent to a prison camp. The only exception is for those found in seaport towns. Those people are "to be kept at hard labour till some of his Majesty's ships coming in or near there give an opportunity of putting them on board, where they shall serve three years under strict discipline, and soldiers pay."[16] Resisters should be "shot as deserters." Locke recognizes that some handicapped people are not capable of the harsh living that takes place on ships. These poor should instead be sent directly to "the next house of correction, there to be kept at hard labour for three years."[17] In effect, the poor are to be forced to work in harsh conditions.

Women and children fare little better than able-bodied or handicapped men. Although one would expect young children to be included in Locke's first category, they are placed in the second. Children older than three and younger than 14 are to be taken by the state and put in a "work school." While Locke recognized that four-year-olds would not be very productive, he saw value in their being trained for a life of work. All children from unemployed households, in Locke's view, who are "above three and under fourteen years of age, whilst they live at home with their parents, and are not otherwise employed for their livelihood" are obliged to go to workhouses.[18] The removal of children to work camps has another benefit for Locke: their mothers would also be freed for work.

Locke is in favour of harsh treatment for all those who resist their work assignments. He is clear that those who either resist work or who are unable to find work are to be forced into prison labour, although it is true that he only suggests imprisonment or harsh labour for those who leave their parish. In effect, he could be suggesting a penalty for loitering. This does not mitigate the harshness of his position, however. After all, those poor who are being targeted could in effect be homeless. They would therefore have no home parish and be forced to wander.

At first there seems to be a major contradiction between Locke's proposal here and the guarantee to a right to "life" that we examined earlier. Is Locke suggesting that the state in effect violate the life of the poor? The proper way of understanding Locke's work provisos so that they do not conflict with the right to life is as punishment for possible infringement on the property of others. The parallels to punishment are made clear by the type of work Locke expects the poor to perform. Ship work during Locke's time was extremely dangerous, and carried with it a high probability of death. Thus Locke proposes prison for the handicapped, since prison (even with hard labour) was a more humane fate than ship work. While imprisonment is obviously punishment, upon closer examination it is a less severe penalty than a Lockean work assignment.

Work as punishment for poverty can furthermore be justified with Locke's view of property. Punishment exists to protect property. If the lazy were allowed to multiply, they would pose a threat to property owners. Poverty often leads to property crime, especially in times of desperation. Without welfare, an economic recession could allow poverty to reach major proportions, potentially overwhelming the capacity of the state to arrest criminals. Punishing the poor before they commit crimes reduces this risk and therefore promotes the state's main goal of enforcing property rights.[19]

Provisos for Those Unable to Work

While Locke believes that work will almost always cure poverty, he seems to provide for minimal relief for the disabled poor. In his testimony, however, Locke indicates that this relief should take the form of charity from the church and the rich; it is not the obligation of a just state. He supports the reading that the right to "meat and drink" is merely a right to work for subsistence. In addition, however, he does provide for a state role in preventing starvation. He argues that although the state should not provide for this subsistence, the state should fine those parishes that allow the poor to starve. Locke argues "that if any person die for want of due relief in any parish in which he ought to be relieved, the said parish [should] be fined according to the circumstances of the fact and the heinousness of the crime."[20]

The right to relief here is not ensured by a state program and thus is clearly not welfare, at least in the modern sense. But Locke does provide for some minimal enforcement of the right. Is this enough to show that Locke mandates welfare payments by private individuals and that therefore the right to "meat and drink" is not entirely private? I believe Locke falls short of making this provision a state entitlement for two reasons. First, no level of subsistence above starvation is guaranteed. Alms could be given in the form of "broken bread" or "other charity." Parishes could avoid the fine simply by giving an individual enough food to stay barely alive. Existence at a level barely above starvation is in no real sense a welfare entitlement. It is more akin to a type of torture.

Second, Locke is clear that the fine is only given after a person dies. There is no provision for state action during the time period in which individuals of a parish sit idly by when an individual is starving to death. The fine offers no guarantee that those unable to work will be kept from starving when they are alive. Rich parishes, after all, could simply agree to pay the fine in return for the right to let an individual die. This ability to buy away entitlements is evidence that Locke does not support a political welfare right.

Conclusion

Locke's theory of property forms the basis for his version of the just state. Since the primary purpose of the state is to protect this property, transfer payments that resemble modern-day welfare are not justified. This is as true for able-bodied and disabled adults as for women and children. Locke does provide for work for the poor, but I have suggested this work is best seen as punishment rather than relief or welfare.

Locke does argue for a right to "meat and drink." But I have argued that this right is a moral, not a political, right. In his terms, it is a "right of Charity" to be provided for by private individuals. Although Locke does oblige the state to fine those parishes that allow starvation, the punishment he suggests is too minimal to give rise to a notion of state entitlement.

Locke's model of distributive justice serves as the primary paradigm that must be attacked for those who want to defend a basic right to welfare. I will suggest that the work of Rousseau serves as such an attack. Specifically, Rousseau's attack on Locke's notion of private property undercuts the libertarian hostility to welfare. Further, I will suggest later on that those philosophers most amenable to the idea of a right to welfare are closely linked to the tradition of Rousseau.

Notes

1   See R. Nozick, *Anarchy, State, Utopia*, for the most well-known of these arguments (New York: Basic Books, 1974).
2   J. Locke, *Second Treatise on Government*, in *Political Writings* (ed. and introduction D. Wootton) (London and New York: Penguin Books, 1993), p. 19.
3   Ibid., p. 9.
4   Ibid.

5   Ibid., p. 31.
6   Ibid., p. 23.
7   Ibid.
8   Ibid.
9   Locke ignores the fact that Native Americans occupied a great deal of this land. It is implicit in his view that in the cases in which people did not farm this land, they did not own it.
10 There are, however, some parallels between punishment and some workfare programs. In some cities, including New York, workfare recipients are made to do public work in clothing that identifies them as workfare recipients. Although the labor is not as harsh as Locke suggested, some might argue that the effect is public humiliation.
11 Ibid., p. 28.
12 I owe this point to Paul Bou-Habib. I would also like to thank Patrick Deneen for his comments on this issue during an informal conversation.
13 Locke as quoted in S. Holmes, *Passions and Constraints: On the Theory of Liberal Democracy* (Chicago: University of Chicago Press, 1995), p. 247.
14 I would like to thank George Kateb for suggesting that I examine this text, in J. Locke, *Political Writings* (ed. and introduction, David Wootton) (London and New York: Penguin Books, 1993).
15 Ibid., p. 447.
16 Ibid., p. 449.
17 Ibid.
18 Ibid., p. 453.
19 Some philosophers, including Mill, have suggested that the poor in effect be paid not to commit crimes as an alternative to forcing work upon them. See Holmes, *Passions and Constraints*, p. 252.
20 Ibid., p. 461.

16   Rousseau and the Fundamental Right to Welfare

Although Locke claims that there is some role for the state in providing subsistence for the poor, the right to welfare is not fundamental in his conception of justice. Those who would seek to establish such a right therefore face the task of showing Locke's theory to be flawed or at least incomplete. Once this is done, advocates of a right to welfare can then move on to show that distributive justice necessitates a guaranteed right to welfare. Jean Jacques Rousseau's political philosophy is worth exploring in depth here because his work aims to accomplish both tasks. He both criticizes Locke's view of property and provides perhaps the first and most complete justification of welfare rights. Before the establishment of the right to welfare can be understood, it is necessary first to explore Rousseau's attack on the notion that property ownership is sanctified by nature. Once we look at this attack on the natural right to property specifically and natural rights in general, we will then go on to examine Rousseau's defense of the notion that rights are grounded in the social contract and, more specifically, in what he labels the "general will." From this conception we are then in a position to understand Rousseau's argument that the right to welfare is fundamental. As we will see, for Rousseau this stance does not necessitate the abolition of private property but rather relies on its existence.

The Attack on Locke

In Rousseau's view, Locke's account of property is both methodologically and ideologically flawed. Locke has attempted, in Rousseau's view, to project a societal concept, namely property, into the state of nature. In Rousseau's view, humans in a natural state could not fathom concepts such as property, much less use them to organize society. Locke's notion of a natural right to property is thus both flawed and dangerous. Locke's methodological mistake serves to reinforce the notion that existing massive inequalities in property are justified. It is only after Rousseau has successfully attacked the natural right to property that he can develop a concept of justice which guarantees the right to welfare. It is therefore worth examining his attack on the state of nature in depth.

Rousseau's attack on Locke's method comes early in his *Discourse on Inequality*. In Rousseau's view, Locke has simply assumed that property and justice existed in nature without showing that humans in such a state would be able to conceive of such concepts. In Rousseau's words, Locke and others "have not hesitated to ascribe to man in that state the notion of just and unjust, without bothering to show that he had to have that notion or even that it was useful to him."[1] According to Rousseau, the concept of justice could not exist in nature. It is therefore nonsensical to look to nature as a guide for a social conception of justice. In order to understand why justice could not exist in nature it is necessary to explore Rousseau's view of the state of nature and concept of language.

For Rousseau, humans in the natural state would have been self-sufficient and therefore would lead asocial lives, without developed social relationships, communities or even language. In nature, Rousseau argues, desires would be quite limited and easily met by individuals. The famous "noble savage" would lead a solitary existence:

> I see him satisfying his hunger under an oak tree, quenching his thirst at the first stream, finding his bed at the foot of the same tree that supplied his meal; and thus all his needs are satisfied . . . When the earth is left to its natural fertility and covered with immense forests that were never mutilated by the axe, it offers storehouses and shelters at every step to animals of every species.[2]

The basic need for food, in Rousseau's account, would be met because, untainted by human development, the earth's resources were unlimited. In addition, because humans would need so little, they could be easily satiated. Rousseau argues that since their needs were all met, there would be no need for humans to form societies. Nature, then, would be characterized by isolated creatures living alone.

The claim of limited needs is important not only because it leads to an asocial lifestyle but also because it means that language could not exist in nature. Since there would be little interaction, no language would develop. A basic language might develop between mothers and their children, but such language in Rousseau's view would end when children were no longer dependents. The claim that there would be no language for humans is also essential for understanding Rousseau's claim that property is not natural. Without language, there could be no "general ideas" or, in other words, any ability to conceptualize. According to Rousseau's view of language, ideas are dependent on the use of language to describe them. Property not only would not exist, but the concept of property could not even be grasped by those in a natural state.

Rousseau's claim might at first seem counter-intuitive. If a woman were stranded on a desert island, alone, she might build a house and a place to cook. Although she might not feel the need to describe these possessions as her property, since there was no one to talk to, she still might feel a sense of ownership. This example, however, assumes that the person who is stranded has a language to begin with. Although technically alone, she is still thinking in terms that she has learned to understand through language.[3] In nature, the noble savage will have no such ability because she has never lived in a social state and thus never acquired language. Therefore, in the state of nature, the concept of property will not only not be useful, but could not even be understood.

The same is true of justice. While the noble savage might fight back if attacked by an animal or another natural human, there would be no way for her to conceptualize the notion that she had been violated or wronged. She would simply fight on instinct without the ability to analyze or label the encounter.

Rousseau attacks Locke for assuming that the first humans had the ability to use language and interact socially. Rousseau's conception of nature, far from being a recognizable society with notions of justice and property, would in fact consist of humans whose behavior brought them closer to the animal kingdom than to modern-day humankind. Since humans in the state of nature would hardly be recognizable, and therefore difficult for social humans to identify with, the question arises: What use does the concept of nature offer us in understanding society? Looking to nature shows us primarily that the concepts we use to regulate our society—for our purposes justice, property and welfare—are originally and totally social concepts. To look to nature for an understanding of these concepts is flawed. Locke's primary mistake was to believe that nature could be used as a baseline from which we could measure the justice or injustice of a given society. As we saw, the law of nature provides the method with which we could examine whether a given state is legitimate or illegitimate. In Rousseau's view, no such law exists.

While nature gives us little help in understanding just property relations, it does provide Rousseau with two principles that any just society will strive for. First of all, it is clear that in nature no individual goes wanting. This will serve as an ideal, in Rousseau's concept of justice. Second, in nature, wants are limited. Rousseau will use this principle to criticize the excessive desires of the rich in society. These principles, while not justified by nature, in which there is no justice, are adhered to in nature. They will inform if not guide Rousseau's social concept of justice.

The Abuse of Justice and Property

The recognition that nature is mostly unhelpful in formulating a conception of justice and property leads Rousseau to reject Locke's method. Rousseau argues that theorists such as Locke have succeeded in using naturalized concepts of justice and property to convince individuals to accept unequal property relations. In fact, in Rousseau's view, there is a widespread acceptance of illegitimate property ownership reinforced by false concepts of justice. Specifically, the term "justice" has been used to justify major inequalities of private property. These inequalities are merely the assertion of the brute force of the rich over the poor.

Before Rousseau can combat these inequalities and create a legitimate system of justice, he first explains why illegitimate concepts of justice and property have been so successful in legitimizing inequality. Specifically, Rousseau argues that there are two reasons why the poor have accepted a situation in which they have almost nothing. First, the instability that came when private property was recognized for what it really was–a brutal assertion of power–was so violent that people were eager to escape it. Second, in Rousseau's view, human psychology is such that the poor were susceptible to the notion that by accepting property relations they would have a chance of becoming wealthy. It is only once these flawed notions of property and justice are understood that it becomes possible to understand Rousseau's own notion of justice and the role welfare plays in it.

Rousseau is clear that the first attempts on the part of the individual to declare his own right to property were brute attempts to exert force over society. Rousseau laments the fact that the individual who first declared "this is mine" in reference to property was not challenged by others:

> What crimes, wars, murders, what miseries and horrors would the human race have been spared, had someone pulled up the stakes or filled in the ditch and cried out to his fellow men "do not listen to this impostor. You are lost if you forget that the fruits of the earth belong to all and the earth to no one."[4]

The claim that one has a right to property is nothing but "a precarious and abusive right" when it is simply claimed by the individual. It is abusive, Rousseau argues, because property is simply taken by force without regard for how its seizure will impact others in the society. As we have seen, no natural sanction justifies the individual simply taking property.

In addition, Rousseau is equally hostile to the Lockean notion that if one labors on the land, he is the only one entitled to its benefits. To those who claim that property is theirs because of their individual labor, Rousseau responds:

By what right do you claim to exact payment at our expense for labor we did not impose upon you? Are you unaware that a multitude of your brothers perish or suffer from need of what you have in excess, and that you needed explicit and unanimous consent from the human race for you to help yourself to anything from the common subsistence that went beyond your own?[5]

Here Rousseau is clear that the individual cannot simply claim private property, even when it is labored upon, because all land and wealth are held in common. While Locke also shared this assumption, Rousseau attacks the Lockean notion that labor entitled one to private property. It is only with the blessing of society at large that an individual is entitled to anything beyond subsistence. Rousseau assumes that individuals who accumulate wealth do so at the expense of other members of society. Excessive wealth, in effect, results in excess poverty.

Despite the fact that the original property grab by those who became rich was illegitimate, Rousseau is clear that it was accepted by society at large. This acceptance, which continues to exist in states with massive inequality, happened for a reason. If the inequalities are to be combatted, an explanation is needed for why illegitimate inequality came into existence.

First, Rousseau argues that originally inequalities in property resulted in "the most frightful state of war." Since it was obvious that property was merely an exercise of power, those who were able continually challenged property owners for their land and wealth. Once one person acquired property, there was little to stop another person who had strength from taking it away. Property owners and non-property owners alike dreaded this instability since violence led to danger for all. As a result, Rousseau argues, rich and poor alike were ready to run into the "chains" of inequality once the rhetoric of justice appeared. Although natural law theories and other conceptions of justice were merely veiled attempts to legitimize the interests of the powerful, a society which craved stability accepted this ideology.

Second, Rousseau argues that there is a fundamental part of human psychology which leads individuals to continually compare themselves to each other. This so-called *"amour propre,"* claims Rousseau, also contributed to the acceptance of an unjust society of inequality. The poor, mistakenly believing that private property relations would give them the chance to also become rich, accepted the rhetoric of justice. The desire for wealth on the part of the poor led to the acceptance of poverty.

For these two reasons the poor were susceptible to the rhetoric of justice. The wealthy took advantage of this vulnerability and in the name of justice convinced the poor to accept inequality:

"Let us unite," he says to them, "in order to protect the weak from oppression . . . Let us institute rules of justice and peace to which all will be obliged to conform . . ."

Considerably less than the equivalent of this discourse was needed to convince crude, easily seduced men who also had too many disputes to settle among themselves to be able to get along without arbiters, and too much greed and ambition to get along without masters for long. They all ran to chain themselves, in the belief that they secured their liberty.[6]

Although the poor accepted this first "illegitimate" social contract, it clearly was instituted on behalf of the rich. It was they, after all who had the most to gain from it. Rousseau reasons that since it was most useful to the rich, they can be seen as the perpetrators of this contract, which is in fact a fraud.

While the acceptance of inequality has led to stability, Rousseau explains that this is not enough to guarantee the existence of justice. In fact, although there is no more fighting, the rich and poor still live in a state of war in which the poor have simply given up. It is implied in Rousseau's writing that the poor would be justified in reclaiming the wealth that was stolen from them by the rich.

We are now in a position to understand Rousseau's critique of the Lockean conception of welfare. For Locke, property ownership is primary and the state has the primary role of enforcing this relationship. While his provisos grant the poor the right to subsistence, this is merely a right to a minimum amount of food, barely enough for survival. As we have seen, it is best regarded as a weak promise of charity. For Rousseau, however, the existence of poverty and inequality in the first place is evidence of injustice. While property relations might seem to be supported by the rhetoric of justice, they are really examples of brute power.

Now that we have explored Rousseau's critique of private property and inequality, we can explore his own conception of distributive justice. Rousseau recognizes that this conception is a social conception not based on a state of nature. In addition, it is fundamentally egalitarian.

Equality, Contract and Welfare

After dismissing Locke's natural conception of justice, Rousseau is left with the task of constructing a view of justice grounded solely in society. The following question arises, however: why would any social conception of justice not simply be an imposition of the powerful? As we have seen, Rousseau is acutely aware of the fact that justice has been abused by the wealthy to justify their own excesses. As we will see, Rousseau distinguishes his conception from illegitimate views of distributive justice by recognizing that he is working with a concept that rests on society's acceptance rather than natural law. In order to gain this acceptance, Rousseau argues that justice must be based in a theory that takes the interests of all citizens into account equally. As we will see, it is precisely this reasoning that will form a solid foundation for the right to welfare.

The claim that justice ultimately rests on acceptance raises the question: if society accepts unequal distribution of property, why is it not legitimate? While people seem to have stopped challenging massive unequal ownership, this does not mean, in Rousseau's view, that they have really accepted it. For one thing, their acceptance rests largely on the notion that there is a fundamental natural right to property. Since their acceptance rests on a false assumption, it is not legitimate. If Rousseau's view is correct, and there is no natural right to property, then his reasoning is sound.

We are left with a situation in society in which a distribution of wealth that people think they accept must be distinguished from a distribution that is really acceptable. In order to create this distinction, Rousseau gives us a notion of agreement or acceptance that is linked to interest. Specifically, Rousseau argues that the only decisions a society can make must be linked to the collective interest of that society. Rousseau labels the social interest of any given society the "general will." Before I examine Rousseau's concept of welfare it is first necessary to explore the general will in greater depth.

For Rousseau, the general will must consist of a unanimous agreement in which the interests of all citizens are calculated equally. As we have seen, this does not mean that all members of a society act as if they are content with their lot in life. Rather, it means that the distribution of wealth in a society, as well as its general condition, must be such that it serves the interests of all. In Rousseau's words, "Each of us places his person and all his power in common under the supreme direction of the general will; and as one we receive each member as an indivisible part of the whole." The fact that the general will is made up of "each member" necessitates that individual well-being cannot be sacrificed for the common good. While the general will determines what is in society's interest, this interest must always tend "toward the conservation of the whole and of each part."[7] The consideration of each individual's interest demands that this interest always be promoted. Societies, that do not protect each of their members' interests, cannot be acting in accordance with the general will, by definition. Their actions are not by unanimous consent and therefore are not just.

The question remains, of course, which conditions satisfy each individual interest and which do not? As we have seen, it is not merely enough to think oneself satisfied with the conditions of a given society. After all, even those who are extremely poor might think they are satisfied or at least feel they have been treated justly. Those who, for instance, believe Locke's theory of the right to property might believe that their own lack of property is justified and that they are only entitled to the bare minimum of food or charity for which Locke's theory provides. While they might not be content, they could be said to accept the system in one sense of the term. This is not enough for Rousseau, however: People cannot simply accept a system that does not serve their interest. Specifically, in Rousseau's view, a polity that allows for extreme inequalities in wealth does not serve the interest of the poorest members of that society and therefore is not legitimate.

If we link acceptance to interest, it is clear why someone in poverty is not having his or her interests served. Why, after all, would anyone agree to live in a condition in which his situation was the bare minimum level of subsistence while others lived lavishly? In some views, Locke's and Hobbes's for instance, the answer lies in the comparison with nature. Life in society is simply better than it would be in nature. However, Rousseau believes such comparisons are useless, as humans in nature do not even resemble humans in society. One's interest is not served in poverty.

Some might make the argument that inequality might benefit the society as a whole. Poverty, while not in the individual interest, it might be argued, is in the general interest. It is precisely this logic, however, that Rousseau is arguing against. The welfare of the individual is by definition linked to the interest of the society. In order to make this point, Rousseau relies on an analogy with punishment. Rousseau argues it would be wrong to allow an innocent man to be punished to serve a social benefit. It would be similarly wrong, he claims, for a society to allow some members of the community to be extremely poor. Allowing this would be akin to sacrificing innocents. The general will, because it must be unanimous, could not allow for either condition.[8] Rousseau asks the reader: "In effect is it not the commitment of the body of the nation to provide for the maintenance of the humblest of its members with as much care as for that of all others? And is the welfare of a citizen any less the common cause than the welfare of the entire state?"[9] The maintenance of a minimum standard of living is therefore indivisible from Rousseau's conception of social justice.

Although massive inequalities of property are not justified for Rousseau, he does not reject the notion of private property altogether. In fact, he declares in *Discourse on Political Economy* that the right is fundamental: "The right to property is the most sacred of all the citizen's rights."[10] There are in fact some distributions of property that Rousseau believes people will legitimately accept. The difference between just and unjust distributions of property lies in the priority that is given to justice. For Locke, property is foundational and justice merely serves to regulate property relations. For Rousseau, however, the relationship is reversed. Property is not grounded for Rousseau in nature and is not assumed to be legitimate. Rather, it must be distributed based on collective interest. If property serves the collective interest, it is accepted and legitimate. If it fails to do so, it is merely an "abusive right." Only property based on such interest could be legitimately accepted. All distributions that do not guarantee a right to subsistence fail to meet this criterion.

While some institutions of property are justified, Rousseau believes it is the state's role to ensure that the distribution of property continually serves the interests of all members of society. In order to ensure this, claims Rousseau, one primary role of government must be to continually redistribute wealth. This should be done first through progressive taxation, in which the wealth of the rich is taken by the government and redistributed to the poor:

> It is one of the most important items of business for the government to prevent extreme inequality of fortunes, not by appropriating treasures from their owners, but by denying everyone the means of acquiring them, and not by building hospitals for the poor but by protecting citizens from becoming poor.[11]

Rousseau's assumption here and elsewhere is that if the government allows for extreme wealth, then extreme poverty will result. As the latter is prohibited by the social contract, so then must be the former.

While Rousseau's argument for the maintenance of a minimum tier above poverty is clear, it is not as obvious why the existence of a wealthy class is not compatible with the general will. After all, what if there is enough money in a given society to both support a minimum tier and yet allow for massively wealthy individuals? Some might even argue that extreme wealth is necessary to support a minimum tier in the first place. If this is true, wealth is not only justified but also necessary to ensure precisely the welfare guarantee Rousseau seems to value. I will deal with these issues when we examine the contemporary work of John Rawls in Chapter 17.

First, however, it is possible to clarify further Rousseau's view of the right to welfare and explore some of the problems that come with his view that such a right is in fact grounded on interest. Specifically, what happens if the theory of redistribution conflicts with what a populace expresses through democratic government? In the United States, there is currently a great deal of hostility toward the right to welfare on the part of the electorate. Although this right is based on acceptance, it seems many do not claim to accept this right. Is Rousseau merely imposing a particular view of welfare and social justice upon a society, all the while pretending to base his theory on acceptance? Furthermore, the charge could be made that Rousseau's view of welfare conflicts with the basic liberties of citizens. After all, Rousseau calls for the active removal of wealth from some members of society. Perhaps such removal is not only counter to popular will but serves as a violation of individual liberty.

The same charges at first do not seem to apply to Locke. For Locke, the state's primary role is one of protection. The state merely serves to preserve existing relations. It interferes only when a citizen's property is threatened.

The conflict between basic rights and democracy emerges here too, however. Consider a circumstance in which the majority of people voted to abolish private ownership altogether. Such a vote would in fact undermine what Locke perceives to be the primary role of the state, namely the protection of private property. In Locke's view, if such a vote occurred and all private property were seized, the state would no longer be justified. Despite the fact that a majority sanctioned the measure, the government would enter into a "state of war" with the population. Democracy, then, is limited to some extent, even by Locke.

A Lockean could argue that this limitation on democracy is acceptable because the state is only limited from interfering with individual liberty. Just as we would want to impose a limit on the majority deciding to murder innocent people, it is also sensible to prevent the state from seizing property. In contrast, a Lockean could argue, the state seizure of property in the name of welfare redistribution is precisely the type of activity that interferes with individual liberty. The violation is all the greater when it is done against the will of the majority. In this case, not only is a majority overruled, but a violation of fundamental liberty has occurred. To sum up, in the Lockean view, democratic rule is limited by the liberty to hold property, a liberty guaranteed by natural justice.

The question remains: does Rousseau's view of welfare demand a sacrifice of both democratic will and liberty? In one common interpretation, Rousseau holds a different view of liberty from Locke. In terms made famous by Isaiah Berlin, the distinction can be made clearer by positing two different "concepts of liberty." The Lockean view can be understood as a defense of negative freedom. Here liberty means freedom from coercion. In terms of negative freedom, one is free to the extent that she is not harmed or imposed on by others. The Lockean state respects this freedom by not seizing an individual's property and by protecting this right against the interference or coercion of other members of this society.

In contrast, Rousseau might be understood to maintain a "positive" conception of freedom. In Berlin's terms, this freedom stems from the urge of individuals to be "masters of themselves."[12] People are free on this view to the extent that they control their own destiny. The question remains, however, what does it mean to be master of one's self? In Berlin's view, some conceptions of the individual lend themselves to the notion that one must be coerced into accepting one's own true self. For instance, consider the view that one is only free to the extent that one is rational. When acting in an irrational manner, one could be said not to be free. Therefore, on a conception of positive freedom, being forced to be rational is equivalent to being forced to be free. Rousseau holds a similar view, but instead of positing the rational self as the true self, he argues that one is free when acting in accordance with the general will.[13] After all, the general will is by definition the true interest of all individuals. To the extent that an individual is forced to act in accordance with the general will, he could be said to be coerced into freedom. To return to the question of welfare, although wealthy individuals or a majority might claim that they do not want the state to transfer wealth to ensure a minimum tier of welfare, forcing them to do so makes them free by Rousseau's standards. Since welfare rights are really in accordance with the general will, society is in fact enhancing freedom when it coerces individuals into providing welfare.

The problems with a positive conception of freedom, especially when applied to politics, are plentiful. For one thing, depending on how society defines the general will, massive coercion could be justified. According to theorists of positive liberty, any protection from coercion would give way to the notion that the state was simply acting in accordance with the general will. Such a view would leave the individual with no protection from the state. While Rousseau uses this approach to justify the right to welfare, it could lead down the slippery slope of tyranny.

Although Rousseau is often read as disregarding negative liberty, it is possible to understand his notion of welfare rights as stemming from a concern with negative freedom. This view becomes clearer on revisiting Rousseau's concept of the right to property. As we saw earlier, such a right is not natural and can only be just when based on the general will. Originally, however, property was simply seized by individuals seeking to advance their own interest. This moment of taking, on Rousseau's view, was a moment of "force" or coercion. By enclosing a plot of land or simply claiming resources as one's own, Rousseau claims, an individual prevents others from sharing in those resources, thereby imposing poverty on others. The institution of welfare rights, then, is merely a way of rectifying original coercion. Just as Locke argued the state would be protecting negative liberty by returning stolen property, Rousseau believes that the establishment of a welfare right restores negative liberty because wealth that originally belonged to all had been stolen by a few.

We are now in a position to understand Rousseau's hostility to the notion that some are entitled to excess wealth. Such wealth is accumulated at the expense of the poor. Since this accumulation is an imposition on the poor, it must be carefully scrutinized. As I have suggested, this view can be supported solely in terms of negative liberty.

The Public Right to Welfare vs. the Private Obligation of Welfare

Now that the views of Locke and Rousseau have been introduced, the question arises as to how their philosophical views relate to the contemporary welfare debate. We have seen that both offer at least some notion of a right to subsistence, but how do they differ in regard to modern welfare provisions?

If we are speaking of moral rights, the difference is one of degree. We have seen that for Locke the right to welfare necessitates that one must have the bare necessities to subsist but nothing more. For Rousseau, however, welfare must guarantee all citizens as much equality as the general will necessitates. As we have seen, since the general will must be unanimous, it will necessitate the elimination of extreme wealth and poverty. Welfare is not merely a right to subsist, but a right to live in a state rooted in an egalitarian system of justice.

A more important difference between the two theorists lies in the role they believe the state needs to play in establishing the political right to welfare. For Rousseau, the right to welfare must be secured by the government and is, in fact, one of the central roles of the state. Rousseauian welfare is perhaps best described as an "entitlement," guaranteed to all simply as a result of their citizenship. For Locke, however, it is less clear who needs to secure the right to welfare. As we have seen, he suggests that the rich have a duty of charity to the poor that can be fulfilled largely through private donations and the church. While Locke argues that this duty must be encouraged by the state, it is hardly the central role of the state. Taxes to redistribute income, in Locke's view, can in fact be seen as a violation of liberty. We are left with two very different justifications of the state and therefore two differing arguments about the state's role in providing welfare payments. As we will see in the next chapter, this historical debate contains the premises inherent in the major contemporary philosophical disputes about the right to welfare. In the following chapters, I will explore how a modern view, that there is a right to welfare, can be found in the philosophy of John Rawls.

Rawls is useful because he provides arguments for many of the claims left unsubstantiated by Rousseau. As we have seen, Rousseau does provide some strong reasons for rejecting the Lockean account of property. In addition, he gives us reason to believe that justice is in fact a social construct. The weakness in Rousseau's theory lies in his failure to explain exactly what justice demands. As we have seen, he claims that such a conception based in the general will would necessitate a basic right to welfare. But how much welfare need a society ensure for all its members in order to institute distributive justice? How much inequality is compatible with such a society? What does it mean to eliminate poverty?

Rawls offers specific answers to these questions and provides arguments for his claims. By exploring these arguments, we will be in a better position to evaluate the results of Rousseau's general will.

Notes

1   J.J. Rousseau, *The Basic Political Writings* (Indianapolis: Hackett, 1987), p. 38.
2   Ibid., p. 40.
3   For a more elaborate discussion of this point see S.A. Kripke, *Wittgenstein On Rules and Private Language* (Cambridge, MA: Harvard University Press, 1982).
4   Rousseau, *Basic Political Writings*, p. 60.
5   Ibid., p. 69.
6   Ibid., pp. 69–70.
7   Ibid., p. 114.
8   Like Rousseau, Kant invokes the notion of the general will in defence of the right to welfare in his *The Metaphysical Elements of Justice*. His language and reasoning echo Rousseau in the following passage: "The general Will of the people has united itself into a society in order to maintain itself continually, and for this purpose it has subjected itself to the internal authority of the state in order to support those members of the society who are not able to support themselves. Therefore, it follows from the nature of the state that the government is authorized to require the wealthy to provide the means of sustenance to those who are unable to provide the most necessary needs of nature for themselves. Because their existence depends on the act of subjecting themselves to the commonwealth for the protection and care required to stay alive, they have bound themselves to contribute to the support of their fellow citizens, and this is the ground for the state's right to require them to do so." The right to welfare here is not a private right to charity. It is clearly a right on the part of the state to tax in order to provide welfare as well as a right of the poor to receive it. (I. Kant, *The Metaphysical Elements of Justice* (New York: Macmillan, 1965), p. 93)
9   Ibid., p. 122.
10   Ibid., p. 127.
11   Ibid., p. 124.
12   I. Berlin, *Four Essays On Liberty* (Oxford: Oxford University Press, 1990), p. 131.
13   Although Berlin labels Rousseau a theorist of positive liberty he also recognizes that poverty can be understood as a violation of negative liberty. Berlin argues that if poverty is actually a human imposition, it can be seen as an impediment and thus a form of coercion. Poverty would then be a violation of negative liberty. The only alternative reading according to Berlin is that poverty is in some ways natural. If this is the case it would not be a result of human coercion but rather a result of natural limitation. Rousseau argued that the former is the case and thus that poverty is a violation of negative liberty.

17 Rawls's Theory of Justice

Central to Rawls's theory of justice is the notion that each citizen's interest must be taken into account equally in any just society. He thus shares two major beliefs with Rousseau. First, both go beyond the claim that equality is limited to equal protection of the laws and embrace the notion that the institutions of society must be structured to serve all citizens equally. Second, for both, the concept that the state must protect the pre-established rights of pre-social individuals is rejected in favor of a view that grounds all rights and the role of the state in a situation of initial equality. As we saw in the previous chapter, these two assumptions lead Rousseau to argue that the maintenance of a substantial social minimum tier was essential in the just society and that massive inequalities of wealth could never be justified. In effect, the welfare of the least well-off was a central concern of the state. For Rawls, the maintenance of the poorest members of a society is also central and, like Rousseau, this position is the direct result of a theory of equality of interests.

Rawls, however, in some ways is more useful than Rousseau in explaining why a welfarist state results from a particular conception of equality because he is meticulous and specific in his arguments. While Rousseau leaves us with the vague concept of the general will, Rawls elaborates on specific principles that result from equality in three important ways. First, using his concept of the original position, Rawls clarifies and provides arguments for the notion that equal interests of what he calls "free and equal" citizens should serve as the basis of a theory of justice. Second, Rawls's arguments are geared to clarifying what type of social welfare policy follows from a position of equality and what types of institutions support such policy. Third, Rawls is concerned to address why his notion of social welfare does not conflict with a justified conception of liberty.

By exploring Rawls's theory, we will be in a much better position to evaluate the view that the legitimate state must provide for a fundamental right to welfare. Rawls's arguments are not only clear but provide perhaps the best contemporary reasoning for such a right. Once we have examined the arguments in detail, we will then be in a position to examine contemporary attacks on the right to welfare. As we will see, theorists such as Robert Nozick build on Lockean notions of property rights and argue that Rawls's theory ignores essential aspects that would have to be present in any society which guaranteed equality. Namely, Nozick claims Rawls fails to give an adequate account of individual rights. I will show that the Rawls/Nozick debate is a contemporary continuation of the tension between Rousseau's welfarist conception of justice and Locke's anti-welfarist conception.

First, however, it is necessary to explore Rawls's arguments in detail. I begin by examining Rawls's concept of equality and its relation to a theory of justice. In his terms, a theory of justice must be a theory of "justice as fairness." This theory demands that all theorizing about just institutions be done from an "original position," in which no one knows their talents or social position. He calls this original position the "veil of ignorance." I then move on to consider why the strategy that will inform the way decisions are made from behind the veil is one that minimizes risk. This strategy leads Rawls to conclude that those behind the veil will choose two specific principles of justice. After examining the content of these two principles, I will then explore why justice as fairness would result in a welfarist conception of the state.

Justice as Fairness and the Original Position

Rawls labels his theory "justice as fairness." This term does not mean, however, that justice simply is that which is fair. For Rawls, there is a distinction between an arrangement which is strictly fair in outcome versus one which is fair in terms of procedure. In Rawls's view, the just society is one which exemplifies founding principles people would agree to in a position of initial fairness. This need not entail that people choose a strictly fair or equal outcome from this initial position of fairness. For example, consider an extremely simplistic situation in which society had one hundred members and one hundred dollars. In such a situation, a perfectly fair arrangement would necessitate that each individual receive one dollar each. In Rawls's view, however, it is not clear that such an arrangement is the one that the individuals in such a society would want if we inquired into their views. They might, for instance, prefer an arrangement in which half the money was distributed and half was invested for the good of all. Perhaps they would want a situation in which all had a chance to win all of the money in a lottery. The point here is that an arrangement which is based on fairness might differ from one in which all decisions were made according to a strict principle of fairness. As we will see, Rawls will argue eventually that, given the choice, members of society would in fact not choose a strictly fair distribution.

Rawls calls such an initial procedure the "original position." The notion of the original position does not mean that there is ever a chance for people to actually choose what type of society they wish to live in. Rather, it suggests a method for determining the characteristics necessary for a society to be just. This method necessitates putting oneself in a hypothetical situation in which one could choose the principles he would wish to live under. The fact that individuals would choose the principles justifies their role as the central basis for the legitimate state. In Rawls's words, "a society satisfying the principles of justice as fairness comes as close as a society can to being a voluntary scheme, for it meets the principles which free and equal persons would assent to under circumstances that are fair. In this sense its members are autonomous and the obligations they recognize self-imposed."[1] The fact that individuals would choose the principles that result from the original position in effect justifies them.

But how could all the members of a society agree unanimously on fundamental principles of justice? Society is ripe with major disagreement on fundamental political issues. Some think the state has the fundamental role of redistributing property. Others believe the state has an obligation to protect current property distribution. How can Rawls expect consensus in a society of dispute? Before it is possible to address these concerns, it is necessary to examine why Rawls thinks that equality in the original position is essential. Once we have understood what Rawls means by equality, we can then return to how consensus can be reached in the original position.

Rawls assumes that each individual must count equally in choosing the principles of justice. If each did not count equally, the decision to adopt the principles would not be a fair one. The notion of justice as fairness, however, is based on the belief that a fair procedure is essential to a just outcome. But how can it be assured that those in the original position are really equal? After all, in a group situation, some parties will be more persuasive and articulate than others and thus perhaps exert a disproportionate influence. Furthermore, these people might advocate their own interests over those who are less articulate and trick others into accepting principles which only benefit themselves. It would seem then that, although all had an equal right to participate in the original position, all interests would not necessarily be represented equally.

Rawls answers that all of those in the original position would have to put themselves behind a "veil of ignorance" in which no one "knows his place in society, his class position or social status, nor does any one know his fortune in the distribution of natural assets and abilities, his intelligence and the like."[2] Those behind the veil of ignorance become representatives for the members of society at large, but because they are stripped of their characteristics, they cannot represent any individual member. As a result, they also cannot attempt to defend their own individual interests. For instance, under the veil, the more articulate members in the original position do not know that they would be more articulate in society. Therefore, it would do them no good to defend principles that would benefit articulate people.

The situation is the same in regard to wealth and social class. If individuals in the original position were aware of their wealth in society, they would often simply advocate positions which would advance the interests of their own social class. If this were the case, it would be nearly impossible for unanimous decisions to be reached in societies which were highly stratified in terms of wealth. Individuals would argue not from a basis of equality, but rather in an attempt to further their own personal interests in society. Here coalitions would be formed with other people of similar means in an attempt to maintain their position; if they were wealthy, for instance, they might oppose welfare transfers to the poor. Likewise, if they were poor, they might be led to support massive welfare transfers. Such bargaining, in Rawls's view, would be arguing from "prejudice" rather than from equality:

> The aim is to rule out those principles that it would be rational to propose for acceptance, however little the chance of success, only if one knew certain things that are irrelevant from the standpoint of justice. For example if a man knew that he was wealthy, he might find it rational to advance the principle that various taxes for welfare measures be counted unjust; if he knew he was poor, he would most likely propose the contrary principle . . . One excludes the knowledge of those contingencies, which sets men at odds and allows them to be guided by their prejudices.[3]

Rawls's language here is telling. Wealth is among the characteristics of individuals in society that are "irrelevant" from the standpoint of justice. Its influence on the thinking of those in the original position is but a residual "prejudice" as it is merely a "contingency." The assumption must be made here that wealth is not a naturally justified trait. If wealth were somehow justified there would seem to be no right to include it among the things that can be discarded in the original position. Since Rawls does not assume that any justification of wealth is valid, he must discount the Lockean notion of natural wealth. Despite Rawls's claims in his later work to offer a "political not metaphysical" theory, it is clear that he must reject at least some, namely Lockean, accounts of the person. While those behind the veil are representatives of people, and Rawls argues they therefore need not resemble actual humans, the fact that some human traits can be alienated in discovering principles of justice commits him to a non-natural conception of justice. This becomes even clearer as we examine the other traits which are irrelevant from behind the veil.

Those attributes traditionally said to lead to the just accumulation of wealth are as contingent as wealth, according to Rawls. On meritocratic views of justice, one deserves wealth due to the particular intelligence or talents with which one is born. If people have the natural intelligence necessary to design brilliant computer programs, they are entitled, some would say, to keep the riches their talents produce. Rawls, however, dismisses this notion in the same manner in which he dismisses the natural right to wealth. Talents, like wealth, are arbitrary from the social point of view. Rousseau's reasoning is helpful here once again in elaborating Rawls's view. While some might have more of a capacity to develop the abilities necessary to be a computer programmer, this capacity must be developed with the aid of social institutions. Without an education which taught these people to use a computer, their potential would never be realized. Further, without a society to produce computers, a talent for computers would be useless. Since talent is only developed in a social context and only of value within the context of social institutions, it is not essentially a natural property and thus cannot be assumed to be of value.

Rawls's insistence that wealth, talent and intelligence are irrelevant in the original position does not, however, exclude the possibility that these characteristics will have a role in the principles of justice. If the participants under the veil of ignorance decide that, for instance, wealth should be linked to a talent for computer programming or that wealth should reward intelligence, such a meritocracy would be justified. Rawls's point is just that these characteristics are not natural and thus cannot be linked to the people who choose the principles of justice. There is nothing, however, which prohibits them from being chosen from behind the veil. As we will see, those who want to argue for a meritocracy have two options open to them in attacking Rawls. First, they can attack the notion that talent, wealth and intelligence are non-natural. Second, if they fail in this, they can argue that such characteristics would be chosen from behind the veil.

While, as we will see, Rawls's claims that talent, wealth and intelligence cannot be assumed in the original position are controversial, perhaps his most contested claim is that effort will also be morally arbitrary from behind the veil. In effect, the participants in the original position will have no idea of whether or not they will be hard workers in society or will want to avoid work altogether. Effort, like wealth, is also morally "arbitrary" according to Rawls. In his view, effort is akin to talent in that both are the combination of birth and social forces. The fact that some might be born with characters which lead them to work hard is not something that should be rewarded, according to Rawls. This fact is a mere accident of birth. The accidental nature of effort is further reinforced by the fact that the talented members in a given society are often rewarded for their talents and therefore led to work hard. Since talent itself is arbitrary, its effects on effort can be seen as arbitrary as well. In addition, Rawls argues that, for many, effort is merely the result of a certain process of socialization. Since many exert effort simply because of the way they were socially cultivated, it seems unfair to assume that effort should be rewarded. As with talent, Rawls argues that people behind the veil are not precluded from valuing effort. However, he argues that it cannot be assumed that those behind the veil will either know how much effort they will put into work or that they will value effort.

Now that we have elaborated on Rawls's notion of equality, we are in a position to understand why he believes those behind the veil can reach consensus on the principles of justice. Stripped of knowledge of who they are in society, those behind the veil all share the same characteristics. Rawls argues that any individual can in effect put himself behind the veil by attempting to shed knowledge of his social position, talents and wealth. The principles that any actor who succeeded in placing himself or herself in this position would choose are the principles all would choose behind the veil.

Now that we have explored the procedure necessary to ensure that just principles are chosen by those in the original position, it is possible to examine Rawls's arguments for the principles of justice that would be chosen. These principles, like the procedure, we will see, are egalitarian and necessitate that the state plays a central role in redistributing wealth to ensure welfare rights.

The Maximin Strategy and the Two Principles of Justice

Once the conditions of the veil of ignorance are accepted, Rawls argues that all people who place themselves behind it will agree that two principles should serve as the foundation of the just society. I will focus in this section on first explaining the strategy Rawls thinks those behind the veil would choose and then examining why they would pick two specific principles of justice. I then explore what impact the principles would have for welfare policy. Specifically, I will argue the two principles lead to a right to welfare.

While we have seen what is necessary for individuals to put themselves behind the veil, the question remains as to how a person in such a position would make choices. The fact that the participants behind the veil will be unaware of their social position, talents, intelligence and effort leads Rawls to argue that they will also be unaware of the specific goals they have in life. In his words, they will be unaware of their own specific concept of the good life. Since knowledge of who people actually will be once they leave the veil is so limited, Rawls argues that discussion behind the veil will be limited to the topic of what all people would want once they left the veil. Since the participants lack the details of the actual lives they will lead, Rawls argues they will prefer to choose principles that would benefit all people. This reasoning leads Rawls to argue that discussion behind the veil will largely be limited to talk of how what he calls "primary goods" will be distributed. Primary goods are defined as those things which all people would want. In Rawls's words "Regardless of what an individual's rational plans are in detail it is assumed that there are various things which he would prefer more of rather than less." These goods will have to be defined broadly and specifically include "rights and liberties, opportunities and powers" and "income and wealth." In addition, Rawls includes "a sense of one's own worth."[4] The argument behind the veil is therefore entirely about distributive justice, broadly conceived. Notice that in addition to traditional concerns of distributive justice like income and wealth, rights are also included in the goods that need to be distributed according to the choice of those behind the veil.

Rawls argues that those behind the veil will all accept the same strategy for the distribution of primary goods. Namely, since no one is aware of who he or she will be in society, all will be averse to risk behind the veil. In fact, Rawls argues that participants will choose the principles which carry with them the least possible risk. The result would be a strategy which always sought to "maximize the minimum" tier of society. Participants behind the veil would assume that they would be part of the group that was least well-off in society. They would therefore be led to choose principles which increase the well-being of this group to the highest level possible. But why would those behind the veil be so averse to risk? Why would they not, for instance, take the chance that they would inhabit the upper reaches of a given society, or perhaps the middle range? Rawls gives two arguments for the "maximin strategy."

First, those behind the veil have no knowledge of either what their society will look like outside the veil or what roles they might play in this society. The veil of ignorance "excludes all but the vaguest knowledge of likelihoods. The parties have no basis for determining the probable nature of their society or their place in it."[5] In effect, they will not even have knowledge of the probabilities that they will inhabit the middle or upper tiers.

Second, Rawls argues that participants behind the veil will not be open to risk the means to pursue their own idea of the good life when they leave the veil. They would perfer to ensure that the minimum tier offers sufficient possibility for them to pursue their concept of the good, than to risk that they might be part of a group which did not have the means to pursue their concept of the good.

The maximin strategy, according to Rawls, will lead the participants to adopt two principles from behind the veil. Rawls claims participants will choose a first principle according to which "each person is to have an equal right to the most extensive basic liberty compatible with a similar liberty for others."[6] In other words, the first principle guarantees a maximum amount of liberty that is distributed equally among citizens. Among these liberties are freedom of speech, conscience, thought, political liberties and the right to own property. Rawls claims that the principle follows a maximin strategy because it guarantees that if one winds up having a concept of the good life which is in conflict with the concept of other members of society, she will want to ensure that her concept is protected. The first principle guarantees that if individuals do have minority status they will be able to pursue their minority concept of the good without interference from the state or others.

Rawls's second principle has two components. The second component states that "offices must be open to all" and in effect is a principle of fair equality of opportunity. It is the first component, which Rawls labels "the difference principle," that is most directly relevant to the welfare question. According to the difference principle, inequalities in primary goods are only justified to the extent that they maximize benefits for the least advantaged. The principle is in effect a direct application of the maximin strategy to the issue of inequalities. At first, it might seem that a maximin strategy would lend itself to a scheme in which all primary goods are distributed equally. Take, for instance, a scheme in which a given society had one hundred dollars of the primary good of wealth. It would seem that given this amount the maximin strategy would necessitate that if there were twenty members of that society each person should receive five dollars. Any inequalities of distribution of the hundred dollars would leave the worse off with fewer dollars than would an equal distribution. If one person were, for instance, given five dollars and twenty cents, the worst off would have at best four dollars and ninety-nine cents, which is less than he would have in a strictly equal distribution.

The above example, however, assumes that the aggregate amount of wealth in a given society is a static zero-sum game situation in which for every increase in wealth there must be a decrease. This is in fact true if the total amount of wealth in a given society never fluctuates. It is possible, however, in theory that the total amount of wealth could increase, which has a direct result of allowing for inequalities in a given society. If, for instance, it so happened that allowing one person to receive an unequal amount of wealth would lead to an increase in the total amount of money in a given society, such an inequality could be justified on maximin grounds. In this case, the inequality could lead to a total increase in wealth which could bring the least advantaged to a point beyond that at which they would be in a situation of strict equality. To return to our example, if one person in a twenty-person society were given twenty of the one hundred dollars, and he could increase the aggregate wealth of a society to two hundred dollars from one hundred dollars, the remaining one hundred and ninety could be distributed equally among the other nineteen people. The result would be a situation in which the lowest tier received a little over four dollars more than they would in a situation without the inequality. This reasoning leads Rawls to argue that a maximin strategy allows for inequalities of primary goods only when they benefit the least advantaged.

We are now in a position to understand why Rawls's theory gives welfare a central role in the just state. The difference principle gives people a right to the maximum amount of wealth possible in a given society simply by virtue of their membership in that society. Since those behind the veil are unaware of their characteristics, they are led to choose principles that benefit the least advantaged, regardless of the characteristics of those in that group. Work is not a requirement, nor is effort. The difference principle goes beyond the notion that welfare is an entitlement to subsistence to the claim that welfare is the right of the least well-off to have the most wealth possible in a given society regardless of one's talent or willingness to work. In Rawls's system, all wealth is distributed not because one has done something to deserve it but merely due to one's membership in society. It is true that effort and talent might lead to increased wealth for society as a whole. To the extent that it is necessary to reward those with these characteristics in order to make them more productive, inequalities can be justified. These inequalities are not justified, however, because work or talent is seen as a good in itself but rather because they can produce wealth to benefit the least advantaged. In effect, work is rewarded only because it maximizes redistribution of wealth to the worst-off.

The difference principle results in the notion that one of the main purposes of the just society is to maximize the amount of welfare payments that are made. For many, a right to welfare merely indicates a right to minimum subsistence in the form of food, shelter and health care. (In even the most liberal interpretation of Locke, he provides for no more than subsistence.) Rawls's right, however, goes far beyond this: in some circumstances the difference principle might lead to something more like a right to live a middle-class lifestyle. Consider, for instance, a society of enormous wealth in which the minimum tier could live at the upper-middle-class level of tenured college professors if the difference principle were implemented.[7] Here the right to welfare really results in a right to be upper-middle class. Once again work or effort is not a factor in attaining this goal.

Some see this example as evidence that the difference principle goes too far in maximizing the minimum tier. Consider what would happen if such a society acquired even more wealth. Strictly interpreted, the difference principle would require that the minimum, although it was already quite wealthy, be increased. Welfare rights would in effect necessitate even greater wealth. Perhaps it could be argued that such a society would be simply wasting its resources at this point. Instead of distributing the wealth to people who already have enough to pursue their concept of the good, perhaps the money should go to promote the arts or to explore space. One might argue that redistribution is sensible in order to provide for a stable baseline, but beyond that, society should spend its money to achieve certain greater goals. Welfare would be secured, but after a basic level of subsistence has been achieved for all, the financial desires of the lowest tier would be trumped by social goals.

In Rawls's view, a concept which limited the difference principle in the manner described above would have to be rejected. In order to understand why this is the case, it is necessary to expand our discussion and compare Rawls's theory with teleological theories of justice. Teleological theories rest on the assumption that there is either one or a collection of values or "goods" that a society should devote its resources to maximizing. Such theories justify social policy as a means of pursuing these goals. An obvious example is the utilitarian theory we explored in the chapter on punishment. There, all punishments were devoted to the good of maximizing pleasure. Although it is less obvious than the case of utilitarianism, the proposal for limited welfare outlined in the previous paragraph is also teleological according to Rawls. Although it posits a principle of welfare which does not necessarily maximize any particular good, the fact that welfare is ultimately trumped by social goals reveals that the theory is at least in part teleological. In order to implement the suggestion that social goods trump the right of the minimum tier to have their primary goods maximized, there must be a shared conception of what constitutes a social good. This, however, is precisely what Rawls's view does not allow for.

In contrast, for Rawls, all policy must ultimately be decided in reference to the principles which have been decided upon behind the veil of ignorance. As we have seen, people behind the veil not only lack knowledge about their particular role in society but about their concepts of the good life. The principles therefore are neutral on the question of ultimate social goods. They merely provide a way to distribute the primary goods that individuals will then use to pursue their own concepts of the good life. While the minimum welfare scheme allows a particular concept of the good to trump the principles of justice, in Rawls's view, the state's obligation to maximize the primary goods held by the minimum tier stems from the two principles of justice which cannot ever be overridden.

The example of the wealthy society reveals that welfare rights are not limited to establishing a stable minimum baseline of society for Rawls. Instead, one's rights fluctuate depending on the amount of wealth in a given society. Rawls's two principles therefore go beyond the establishment of a minimum tier of subsistence. The term "welfare" is often used in contemporary debates, especially those in the realm of electoral politics, to refer to the attempt to secure basic needs. Welfare defined as such could be termed "needs welfare."[8] It is perhaps worth asking whether the difference principle, which is not based on needs, in fact leads to a concept of welfare. Is a scheme which demands maximizing the minimum well beyond basic needs, perhaps to the point of middle-class stability, really an argument for welfare? If welfare is by definition needs welfare, the answer is clearly no. But it is unclear why welfare must be inherently tied to needs. If in fact welfare is a basic right, it would seem that the justification of rights rather than needs would provide its basis. The difference principle is foundational for Rawls, and according to this principle, the right to be maintained at as high a level as possible is an entitlement linked to justice, not needs.

Perhaps it will be objected that rights do not by their nature fluctuate in the way that the income level of the minimum tier in society does. The right to welfare, if it is needs welfare, would always guarantee a specific level of subsistence, whereas income distributed according to the difference principle continually changes depending on the amount of wealth in a given society. In this sense, the difference principle does not necessarily establish a right. This point could be illustrated in reference to a society which is quite poor. Perhaps in such a society the difference principle would not guarantee even minimum welfare rights. If such a society maximized the minimum tier but was too poor for this maximization to fulfill health care needs, for instance, it would seem to comply with the difference principle, yet fail to establish a right to welfare at the level of subsistence. The right guaranteed by the difference principle in this society would be quite inferior to the right which stems from the difference principle in the society of professors.

Rawls readily concedes the point that the two principles do not specify an exact or stable amount of welfare distribution: "In fact, the principles of justice do not even mention the amount or the distribution of welfare but refer only to the distribution of liberties and the other primary goods."[9] While the right to welfare–defined as adequate resources–is not directly specified by the two principles, it is more than met as a direct result of the difference principle in cases of wealthy societies. As we have seen in these cases, the difference principle provides for more than adequate survival. The question remains, however: is welfare secured in the case of the poor society? While the difference principle might guide the actions of the poor society, it might not be sufficient to ensure that there are enough total resources in a given society which has a low aggregate amount of wealth. In this sense, the difference principle might guide a society but not guarantee welfare.

Consider, however, a society which was similarly poor but guaranteed welfare rights based on needs welfare rather than as a result of the difference principle. In such a society, welfare rights would be guaranteed in theory but not in practice. Here the right might serve as an impetus to the society to increase its total wealth and then redistribute enough to ensure basic needs are met. But why can the difference principle not function in a similar way? There is no reason to think that simply because a society redistributes to a minimum tier it is complying with the difference principle. The principle demands not only that wealth be distributed but that the minimum tier be "maximized." The process of maximization necessitates an increase in total wealth in order to raise the minimum tier.

We are now in a position to answer the charge that the difference principle does not secure a right to welfare because it seems to fluctuate. I would like to suggest that two questions need to be asked in order to determine if a society has complied with the difference principle. First, has it distributed its resources to maximize the minimum given its actual aggregate wealth? Second, has it pursued a policy of aggregate growth, which will result in an increased maximization of the minimum tier? If welfare rights are tied to the first question, they are not adequately guaranteed and fluctuate greatly given the particular society. If welfare rights, however, are tied to the second question, they can be understood as principles which are continually being pursued by a given society. Here the amount at which the actual right is secured will vary with the success of a given society. Wealthier societies that implement the difference principle will have succeeded in granting welfare rights to a greater extent than those societies which have low total aggregates of wealth. Here the difference principle is conceived as an impetus to the achievement of welfare rights.

While the notion of a fluctuating right is not inimical to the very concept of rights, on the libertarian view the notion of a right to welfare is nonsensical. Rights, libertarians argue, are protections from the state. Since welfare is granted by the state, they argue, it cannot be a right. I explain in the next section why, for Rawls, all rights stem from the initial position and why the distribution of primary goods and welfare, while not a liberty defined solely by the first principle, is a right essential to a concept of justice.

Welfare Rights, Liberty and the Difference Principle

In the previous section I discussed why welfare rights stem from the difference principle. While it is clear that the difference principle leads to a specific conception of the distribution of wealth, it still needs to be established that the results of that distribution can be called rights and specifically welfare rights. Libertarians in the tradition of Locke will especially contest the notion that there could be a welfare right at all. Liberty in that tradition is meant to secure rights that pre-date the existence of the state. In fact, the state is one of the major entities from whom individuals must be protected. In contrast, the "rights" that stem from the difference principle must be secured by the state through a system of redistribution. In fact, this redistribution is one of the central roles of the state. In this sense the welfare rights I have been describing are not rights of protection but of intervention. Since rights are by definition the means by which we secure liberty, it is necessary to show that welfare rights, which are dependent on state intervention, do secure liberty rather than interfere with it. The question remains: does the egalitarian distribution necessitated by the difference principle infringe upon liberty?

This question can be formulated as a problem within Rawls's own theory of justice. As we have seen, Rawls posits the first principle as one primarily about liberty and the second as one at least in part about redistribution. The possible problem arises with Rawls's additional requirement that the liberty principle is "lexically prior" to the second principle. In other words, in instances where the two conflict, the former trumps the latter. As we have also seen, Rawls posits the right to property as one of the liberties ensured by the first principle. The question arises: does the redistribution of wealth necessitated by the second principle conflict with the right to property that is part of the first? One initial response might be to claim that the first principle itself ties liberty to equality. After all this principle does justify a right to equal liberty. Perhaps the right to property is actually a right to equal property. The fact that this right would have to be distributed by the state is not a problem for Rawls. After all, as we have discussed, "liberty" itself is a good, the distribution of which must be justified from behind the veil of ignorance. Liberties, like all goods, must be grounded in a conception of justice dependent on the distribution decisions of those in the original position. The right to equal property is not therefore a violation of the right to own property, because all liberties and rights are distributed from behind the veil.

Strictly speaking, Rawls does not, however, provide a guarantee to equal property. The inequalities of the difference principle create inequalities of property. As a result, the right to welfare is not a right to own equal amounts of property. Rather, it demands that people accept unequal distributions to the extent that these distributions benefit the least advantaged. The right to welfare is dependent on the maximin strategy of the difference principal. But do the resulting inequalities not violate the equality component of the first principle?

In order to understand why Rawls's answer to the above question is in the negative, it is first necessary to grasp his notion of the "worth of liberty." Although the first principle necessitates that government protect liberties among its citizens equally, Rawls recognizes that those who have more access to primary goods will be able to use their liberties more effectively than others. These people do not have more liberty than others do. Rather, Rawls claims, for them the "worth" of their rights and liberties is greater. Primary goods therefore serve as tools that aid people in taking advantage of their rights. In regard to property rights, unequal worth of liberty is justified in the same way that the difference principle is justified. The worth of the liberty to own property is unequal in a situation in which inequality of wealth is legitimate, but this inequality is legitimate because those at the bottom of the society have more worth of liberty than they would in a society which distributed property equally.

The right to property is therefore a right that has different amounts of worth for different people. These inequalities are justified, however, because they benefit the least advantaged. To the extent that welfare rights result from the difference principle, they can be seen as a guarantee that the inequalities of worth of property serve to maximize the interests of the minimum tier.

Since for Rawls all principles are grounded in the equal situation of the veil of ignorance, rights are not limited to protections of individuals from government. They do not pre-exist society but rather stem directly from the interests of its members. Rights, then, in some sense are all socially grounded. The result is that a right to welfare can stem from the basic principles in much the same way that more traditional rights can.

The question remains as to what a right to welfare will actually mean for Rawls. So far it has become clear that such a right entails a government obligation to provide as many primary goods as it can for the minimum tier. The question remains, however, as to how these rights are to be enforced. Is the legislature solely responsible for guaranteeing the maximin right to welfare? Should such a right be guaranteed by the constitution? I will return to this question in a later section. First, however, I want to look at some criticisms of Rawls's defense of the right to welfare.

Notes

1   J. Rawls, *A Theory Of Justice* (Cambridge, MA: Belknap Press of Harvard University Press, 1971), p. 13.
2   Ibid.
3   Ibid., p. 19.
4   Ibid., p. 92.
5   Ibid., p. 155.
6   Ibid., p. 60.
7   I owe this example to a conversation with Amy Gutmann.
8   I return to the notion of needs welfare in a later section on Michael Walzer's *Spheres of Justice: A Defense of Pluralism and Equality* (New York: Basic Books, 1983).
9   Rawls, *Theory of Justice*, p. 327.

18 Walzer and the Critique of Primary Goods

We have seen in Chapter 17 that Rawls's difference principle makes redistribution an essential aspect of the just state. Precisely how, however, will the difference principle operate in practice? Does it offer a guarantee of basic needs such as food and shelter? In this chapter, I examine a criticism of the Rawlsian view that welfare guarantees are the result of the just distribution of primary goods. Specifically, I focus on an alternative to the notion of primary goods presented by the political philosopher Michael Walzer. I argue that this alternative poses a challenge to Rawls's view of welfare.

In *Spheres of Justice*,[1] Walzer argues that welfare cannot be discussed outside of the context of a particular society. Specifically, he argues that societies develop "social meanings" for what he calls a "plurality of goods." Whereas Rawls's discussion of material wealth is largely limited to the "primary good" of income, which in turn is used to purchase other goods, Walzer focuses on the wide variety of material goods and services themselves–for example, healthcare, food, shelter, and luxury goods. It is only by discovering the social meaning of each good through examining the social systems of a given society that it becomes possible to discuss what a just distribution might entail. Although *Spheres of Justice* does not contain an explicit attack on Rawls, it is possible to derive a critique of Rawls through Walzer's approach. The critique can be divided into two parts. First, Rawls fails to recognize that a plurality of goods existing in a society cannot be reduced to simply "those things which everyone would want," or, in Rawls's terms, to "primary goods." Second, Rawls fails to understand and use current practices to justify welfare. Instead, by relying on the veil of ignorance, Rawls's project is based in an abstraction distanced from the actual way communities function.

Before we can develop Walzer's first criticism, it is necessary to understand why Rawls's theory leads to a monolithic conception of social goods. Rawls's view of welfare is compatible with the notion of a national guaranteed income.[2] If all people were given enough money directly from the government to satisfy the maximin principle, they could secure their basic needs without services

125

from the government. Given this opportunity, many people would devote their income first to health care, shelter and food. Consider, however, the person who decided that he would rather sacrifice some basic necessities–health care, for example–in order to devote his resources more fully to pursuing his own particular concept of the good–dining in fancy restaurants, for instance. In Rawls's scheme, although the basic income might be enough to provide for basic needs, there is no guarantee that some people would not choose to sacrifice some of these necessities for luxuries. Because of his insistence on providing the means to fulfil basic needs rather than on ensuring that the needs are in fact met, Rawls seems to allow for situations in which some basic welfare provisions are not secured. Primary goods are used in a monolithic form of distributive justice; the government distributes them so that they can then be used by individuals to purchase a plurality of goods.

According to Walzer, the notion that the state should provide funds that could be used for fine dining at the expense of health care is counter-intuitive. Welfare is meant to provide relief, not to subsidize luxury. In his view, Rawls's focus on primary goods conflates the different "spheres" of a given society and distorts the social meaning of the particular goods in those spheres. Specifically, as Walzer sees it, welfare occupies a distinct sphere of life with its own logic. Within the sphere of welfare, there is a plurality of goods, each intertwined with a specific individual need. The good of health care, for example, should be distributed according to need because health care is really about making people healthy. Individuals do not deserve health care because they are wealthy but rather because they are in need of being healthy.

In contrast to health care, to return to our previous example, dining in fancy restaurants is not within the sphere of need. It would seem silly to claim in our society that an individual "needs" to eat at the Four Seasons in the same way he would need an operation for a hernia. In Rawls's account, however, primary goods can be used as one wishes. Needs are no more fundamental than fine dining because individuals can spend primary goods in the manner in which they choose. For Rawls, we do not have a right to health care so much as an ability to purchase it if we so choose. In Walzer's theory, however, the need for health care, shelter and food is simply more fundamental than fine dining. Choice, according to Walzer, should not be a component of the state's obligation to secure basic needs.

In response to Walzer's critique, a Rawlsian might counter that the realm of freedom should include the right to sacrifice one's basic welfare for luxury. While the right not to seek treatment might be fundamental, Walzer could respond to this claim that the Rawlsian scheme allows people to cut off future possibilities of pursuing treatment. If I forgo my operation, spending all my primary goods eating out, and then find myself in great need two days later, I cannot suddenly choose to spend my primary goods on the operation after all; they have already been spent. Walzer's scheme ensures that health care is dependent on the degree to which one needs it, not caprice, and is thus always an option.

Walzer's view does seem grounded in our common practices in a way which Rawls's is not. In our current society, we distribute welfare based on need. Medicaid is meant to provide a safety net for those who do not have health care. Food stamps are meant to ensure that everyone has the ability to meet the basic need to eat. Rawls's notion of the veil of ignorance demands that we abstract from the way we actually conceive of welfare–namely as a method for distributing goods that are necessary for subsistence. Is Walzer not simply justifying our practices by reporting on what we actually do? His view seems open to the charge that he is merely offering a defense of the status quo.

In response to this charge, Walzer could argue that our practices offer an insight into the type of community we would like to live in, not just a reflection of our current community. Our society, he could argue, really believes that health care is relative to need, not personal financial circumstances. Although our current system only partly reflects this intuition (in the United States, for instance, there is no universal health care), the belief is still deep-seated. For example, this belief is revealed in the fact that we do not allow individuals to sell their organs. The link between health care and need, and food and need, is both reflected in our practices and forms the basis for critiquing the status quo. Walzer's critique, however, comes from within the community and is not simply abstract philosophical speculation.

In response to Walzer's view, Rawls could argue that his welfarist conception has a much greater regard for a deeply held value in liberal societies: personal autonomy and liberty. Specifically, Rawls is concerned with providing for a distribution of goods in which all have the ability to pursue their own private conception of the good. By failing to specify what that good is, government ensures protection of individual liberty. Since Walzer bases welfare on specific needs, he fails, Rawls might argue, to respect individual autonomy. If an individual has a concept of the good which does not demand a focus on health, why, Rawls might argue, should the government only offer welfare provisions that he or she might not want?

In conclusion, Walzer offers two criticisms of Rawls's notion of primary goods. First, it allows individuals to give up their basic right to have welfare distributed according to need. Second, it does not reflect the way welfare is understood in our actual society. In his defense, Rawls might point to the liberty present in his account that is lacking in Walzer's.

Notes

1   M. Walzer, *Spheres of Justice: A Defense of Pluralism and Equality* (New York: Basic Books, 1983).
2   The one good that cannot be met with a basic income is the primary good of self-esteem. Rawls devotes little time to discussing this primary good. Further it is not clear that this good is relevant to welfare policy.

19   Rawls, Work and the Free-rider Problem

Rawls's view of effort, discussed in Chapter 17, strikes many as counter-intuitive. As we saw, Rawls theorizes that work should not determine income. Although Rawls does allow for some instances in which one's effort could lead to increased personal benefit–for instance rewarding effort with an increased salary if this will maximize the minimum tier–effort is not rewarded because it is valuable in itself. Rather, work is tied to income because it benefits the lowest tier, including those who do not have a job. For Rawls, there is no essential link between work and income.

This view that work should not be directly tied to income raises what philosophers call the "free-rider problem:" Why should a society support those members who provide no benefit to that society and merely drain its resources? A Rawlsian could offer a first response framed in terms of capability. Some, it could be argued, simply do not have the ability to work due to physical or mental limitations. Yet these people are still members of our society. Further, a Rawlsian could argue that those behind the veil, not knowing whether they might suffer from these limitations, would not risk creating a society in which income would be denied those incapable of working.

But what defense can a Rawlsian offer for providing income to those who are capable of working but simply choose not to? In Rawls's account, the notion that anyone chooses to lack effort is simply false. Rawls argues that no one any more chooses whether they will be prone to put a lot of effort into work than they choose their natural talents:

> The extent to which natural capacities develop and reach fruition is affected by all kinds of social conditions and class attitudes. Even the willingness to make an effort, to try, and so to be deserving in the ordinary sense is itself dependent on happy family and social circumstances.[1]

Effort, he argues, is simply a disposition that develops as a result of one's contingent cultural circumstances. Furthermore, there is an additional connection between talent and effort. It is often the case that those who are praised often early in life because of their natural talent want to work hard as adults. If effort is socially motivated, however, why not design a culture in which people are motivated to work? The fact that some would be motivated to work simply as a result of such a policy reveals that even if effort is not a choice, it can be instilled in individuals. But such a policy still leaves the problem of the free rider unresolved. What happens if after an incentive program, some still refuse to work? Society might not, in fact, always be capable of creating effort. As a result, the Rawlsian could state that no one behind the veil would risk becoming one of those people who could not be brought through social motivation to work. While creating incentives to work is compatible with the Rawlsian project, demanding work to receive a minimum income is not.

Many theorists are unsatisfied with the Rawlsian response to the free-rider problem. Amy Gutmann and Dennis Thompson propose an alternative approach to the problem in their book *Democracy and Disagreement*. In their view, income must be distributed in accordance with a principle of reciprocity. Income is distributed to those who participate in a society. For those who are able, working is a necessary way to participate. The authors, however, are clear to point out that employment opportunities must be made available for those who want to work. Further, the rewards that are given for work must be at a standard of decency: "The obligation of welfare should be mutual: citizens who need income support are obliged to work, but only if their fellow citizens fulfill their obligation to enact public policies that provide adequate employment and child support."[2] In the view of Gutmann and Thompson, citizens must work, but the government needs to ensure that work is fairly rewarded and available.

Gutmann and Thompson argue that before guaranteed welfare can be eliminated, the government must assure that those who do work have the means to live decent lives. Specifically, they argue, the government must ensure "universal health care, universal child care, job placement services, public transit, a higher minimum wage, better unemployment insurance and more sex education."[3] While government responsibility to those who do work is great, it does not extend, in their view, to those who choose not to work despite the fact that they are capable. As they see it, people have the right to surf all day, but the state has no responsibility to support such people because they in effect refuse to participate in society: "If they choose to spend their life surfing at Malibu, they cannot reasonably expect their fellow citizens to support them."[4] Gutmann and Thompson's principle of reciprocity places demands on both citizen and state.

In response to those who would use the critique from reciprocity as an argument for workfare, Rawls, I believe, could argue that it is necessary to place those who "refuse" to work in the appropriate larger social context. Those who seem unwilling to work have at times been raised in an environment which lacks the social support received by those who are willing to work. Consider the example of an individual who was abandoned by her family at a young age and lived on the street throughout her childhood. If her life were examined at one point in time, she might be judged to lack effort and the willingness to participate in society. But this lack of effort would be a direct result of the neglect she had suffered throughout her life. If we were to judge such a person's right to welfare based solely on her effort at one point in time, we would in effect ignore the harmful way she had been treated as a child.

If, however, Gutmann and Thompson's view of reciprocity is applied to evaluating individuals over the course of a lifetime, their view can be reconciled with Rawls's view.[5] Rawls offers a view of obligation that incorporates one's entire life history. He argues that while all have a natural duty to uphold the principles of justice, those who have benefited most from the distribution of wealth take on special "obligations." Rawls claims it is sensible for a society to require more from those who have been given a great deal than from those who have been given little. The advantage of this principle is that it does not require reciprocity from those who have been disadvantaged throughout their lives. As a result, Rawls's principle of obligation does not necessitate the abandonment of the notion of a basic income. Those from whom society can expect a lot are those at the top of the income scale.[6] Those who receive the social minimum have little expected of them because they have not received the bulk of the benefits society has to offer.

The Rawlsian view of reciprocity does not, however, solve what has become known in the literature as the problem of the Malibu surfer.[7] Suppose that a person who has been raised with wealth and love decides to spend her entire life surfing off Malibu and refuses to work or contribute anything to society. Such a person, in contrast to the person from the minimum tier, has been given all the benefits of society but gives nothing back in return. Rawls, and Gutmann and Thompson, would condemn those among the "super-rich" who benefit from the wealth of society and yet choose to live a life of leisure like the surfer. The impact of this application of reciprocity is unclear on welfare policy, however. Such an argument could lead to the conclusion that massive taxes on such a leisure class are justified. What, however, is the impact of such a principle on welfare policy? I suggest not very much. It is possible to posit a hypothetical privileged surfer who was cut off from her wealthy family for her slothful ways. However, such examples are few and far between. Very few welfare recipients fit this description, and it would be difficult, if not impossible, to target such individuals regardless of whether they deserve government support. On the Rawlsian account of reciprocity, therefore, those policies which threaten to cut off those on welfare if they refuse to work would not be justified.

For Rawls, those who do not work cannot be denied the benefits of the two principles. In his account, those behind the veil will be too risk-averse to allow for a society in which some people are cut off from benefits. He does, however, offer some account of reciprocity. Those who have been given a great deal from society have "obligations" not required of those who have been given little. Those who believe effort is not as socially constructed as Rawls claims, or who retain a belief that all should work regardless of class and personal background, will not be satisfied with the Rawlsian solution to the free-rider problem.

Notes

1   J. Rawls, *A Theory of Justice* (Cambridge, MA: Belknap Press of Harvard University Press, 1971), p. 74.
2   A. Gutmann and D. Thompson, *Democracy and Disagreement* (Cambridge, MA: Belknap Press of Harvard University Press, 1996), p. 276.
3   Ibid., p. 280.
4   Ibid.
5   In conversation Amy Gutmann has suggested that such an application would be consistent with her view of reciprocity.
6   Here there is a good deal of overlap on this point between Rawls, Gutmann and Thompson.
7   This example is discussed by Gutmann and Thompson and was posed by Philip Van Parijs. See Parijs, "Why Surfers Should Be Fed: The Liberal Case For An Unconditional Basic Income," *Philosophy and Public Affairs*, 20 (Spring 1991), pp. 103–105.

20   Nozick, Desert and Natural Talent

In addition to the concerns about effort and work raised by fair-workfare views, Rawls's account of natural talent as unacceptable is attacked from another ideological direction. According to the libertarian view, it is not enough to claim that effort is a morally significant trait that needs to be linked to desert. Libertarian theorist Robert Nozick argues that the rewards one derives from his or her particular natural talents are also morally deserved by those who own them. For the state to deny individuals the rewards of their talents is equivalent to theft.

Nozick argues that Rawls's notion that talents are morally arbitrary is fundamentally flawed. As we have seen, for Rawls, natural talents are not known behind the veil of ignorance because they are arbitrary from the moral point of view. Furthermore, those behind the veil would not approve of a system of distributive justice that gave moral significance to natural talents, because they would risk lacking such talent outside the veil.

Nozick argues in *Anarchy, State, and Utopia*[1] that it does not follow from Rawls's view of natural talents that no one deserves the benefits of their talents. While Nozick is willing to grant Rawls the point that individuals have done nothing to deserve their natural talents, in Nozick's view, this point alone is not enough to prove that talents are morally irrelevant to the amount of goods an individual deserves. To use his example, the mere fact that one of "many sperm cells succeeds in fertilizing the egg cell is (so far as we know) arbitrary from a moral point of view" does not lead to the conclusion that the end result of that interaction–namely, a human being–is arbitrary from the moral point of view. In the same way, although people do not deserve their talents, it does not follow that they do not deserve the results of those talents.

While Nozick is correct in asserting that some morally insignificant objects have the potential to cause morally significant objects to come into existence, it is not clear why this leads to the conclusion that natural talents should be rewarded. In Nozick's sperm example, a life results from a long chain of causal events. The case of talents, however, is distinct from one of pure causality.

Reward is not a biological result of talent in the way that life is the result of sperm. A society confers reward and has the option of determining whether or not it is given for significant reasons. The same is not true of the progression from sperm to life.

Nozick is on somewhat firmer ground when he argues that Rawls's notion of natural talents leads him to neglect what he calls the "distinctness of persons." While natural talent might rest in individual persons, in Rawls's view they can only be developed or not developed to the extent that they improve the welfare of the least well-off. As a result, Nozick argues, Rawls winds up turning individual traits into a social commodity. As Nozick sees it, because one's talents make up her personality, to be respected as a distinct person, she must be allowed to keep the results of her talents.

Nozick's claim has two flaws. First, the notion that talents could have any value outside of their social value is quite doubtful. Even if it is true that some talents are the direct result of natural forces, they are only worth anything in the context of a given society. While one might have the natural propensity to be a great stockbroker, this "talent" would be worthless if there were no stock market to give value to that talent. Natural talents are recognized only because of a given social context, and it is society that confers value upon these traits. The claim that talents make individuals distinct in that given social context does not lead to the conclusion that they naturally deserve the results of those talents.

Second, Nozick assumes that taking the results of a particular talent would be the equivalent of denying the distinctness of persons. Why, however, could a society not praise an individual for his contribution to the creation of social goods and then proceed to redistribute them? In other words, the recognition that one person has a talent which produces social goods, does not entitle that person to keep those goods.

Nozick concludes that individuals deserve the fruits of their talents and labor. Furthermore, he believes that this means that any attempt to take one's gains and redistribute them is a violation of a basic principle of desert. I have argued that the fact that talents exist does not mean that individuals should be rewarded for having them.

Note

1   R. Nozick, *Anarchy, State, Utopia* (New York: Basic Books, 1974).

21 Should There be a Constitutional Right to Welfare?

Throughout Part II, we have been concerned with the degree to which welfare provisions are justified or necessitated by conceptions of distributive justice. We have not yet addressed the question of how welfare is to be secured if it is in fact essential to a concept of justice. In this chapter, I explore whether welfare provisions should be secured by a written constitution and enforced by courts engaged in the process of judicial review.

The answer to the above questions for libertarians such as Locke and Nozick would be a clear no. For these theorists, liberty includes the protection of individual property from the state. In their view, systems of welfare that necessitate the distribution of wealth to the degree that Rawls and his followers demand violate property rights. Since massive redistribution leads to unjust taking, welfare clearly should not be protected by a constitution.

While all citizens in the United States certainly do not embrace the libertarian position, the US Constitution is commonly seen as offering primarily libertarian guarantees. Namely, the Constitution protects individuals from government interference but does not necessitate that individuals be provided with material goods. This distinction can be explained by the difference between "formal" and "material" rights. Formal rights are protections of the negative freedom to do as one pleases without external coercion. To the extent that the government does not prevent a woman from getting an abortion, she has the formal right to do so. A material right, by contrast, gives people the actual ability and means to exercise their right. Although one has a formal right to an abortion, if she lacks the money to pay for the procedure, she might lack the material ability to do so. If the government were to ensure material rights, it would have to provide the means to exercise the freedom to have an abortion.

As I have shown, libertarians would argue that the proper role of any constitution is to protect formal rights, not material rights. A government that taxes its citizens in order to ensure that all of them have the means to exercise their rights is violating the formal right to keep one's own property. But what is the proper role of a constitution for a Rawlsian? Should it provide material as well as formal rights?

In Rawls's notion of the value of liberty, both material and formal rights are essential to a conception of justice. To recap, the first principle provides for a right to property, but this right is only given value when the difference principle provides for a distribution of primary goods that will ensure that property distribution always maximizes the minimum tier. A conception of justice which merely protected property without enacting the difference principle would in effect be ensuring liberty that had no value. It is only when the right to property is given value by the second principle that a society can be labelled just. Rawls, then, unlike the libertarian, cannot accept the notion that formal rights are more important than material rights. The question remains, however: even if material rights are essential to a conception of justice, should they be written into a constitution?

In *Political Liberalism*,[1] his follow-up to *A Theory of Justice*, Rawls himself indicates that the answer is no. While the difference principle is essential to a theory of justice, the legislative branch best secures it, Rawls argues. This is true largely for technical reasons. Both the results demanded by the difference principle and the method for bringing about these results are ambiguous. What system of taxation would best maximize the minimum? What rule of torts and property would bring about the maximin result? These questions, Rawls indicates, are too technically complex to be left to an elite panel of judges.

It is unclear, however, why some aspects of the difference principle, if not the principle in its entirety, could not be included in a constitution. For instance, a constitutional standard which necessitated that all members of a given society be provided with enough goods to ensure an adequate standard of living would not be as technically complicated as a provision which required the enforcement of the key aspects of the difference principle by the court. Call this the "adequate standards provision." The adequate standards provision could call for all citizens to have the goods necessary to live a good life, choose among a range of good lives, and participate as equals in their society.

The adequate standards provision would not transfer the entire difference principle into a constitution, but it would establish a minimal welfare level consistent with the difference principle. The provision would also avoid the technical difficulties associated with completely implementing the difference principle. Using the more minimal standard, the court would merely have to judge whether or not resources were distributed evenly enough to allow all to pursue the good life.

A constitution that guaranteed welfare rights would protect those who have been the victims of unjust inequalities in wealthy countries. In examples where enough wealth to ensure a decent minimum tier existed in society as a whole but where massive inequality existed, the court, acting in accordance with a constitution that ensured welfare rights, would demand that the state begin the process of redistribution. Here, the policy might not be implemented immediately, but the court could serve as an impetus. For example, the court could demand that health care be provided in a rural village, although it might take time to build facilities.

The case is more complicated in poor societies. We can imagine a situation in which the court guaranteed adequate standards, but in which the society as a whole was too poor to ensure such rights. In these cases, welfare rights could be seen as ideals for which the court would advocate. The court's demands would not immediately be acted upon in this case, but the court would serve as an impetus for enough economic growth to ensure the guarantee of welfare rights. At the same time, it would serve as a protection against the seizure of economic gains by an elite.

The adequate standards principle therefore offers a constitutional guarantee that avoids the complexities that would come with the court's enforcing a total maximin strategy. It provides for the guarantee of a minimum tier that could be enforced by the court without excessive meddling in policy decisions.

Note

1   J. Rawls, *Political Liberalism* (New York: Columbia University Press, 1996).

22   Marx and the Radical Critique of the Right to Welfare

Thus far in Part II, we have examined the question of whether or not there is a fundamental right to welfare in the legitimate and just state. I have shown that there is massive disagreement on this issue. Welfare rights are central for theorists such as Rousseau and Rawls, whereas they play at best a tangential role for others such as Locke and Nozick. Despite the tension between these welfarist and anti-welfarist camps, all of the theorists we have examined in this part are vulnerable to a common attack from the Marxian left. Marxists, and as I will show in this chapter, Marx himself, would object to the basic vocabulary that all of these thinkers share. Specifically, all of the thinkers we have examined assume that through the language of justice, rights and equality, it is possible to theorize about and eventually reach a state that is legitimate. In the Marxian view, however, this assumption is flawed. Terms like "justice" and "rights," which I call juridical terms, remain rhetorical devices that preclude rather than bring about real liberation. By focusing on juridical terms, according to the Marxian thinker, theorists only succeed in hiding the brute fact that the state is an instrument of the powerful used to keep the weak in bondage.

This attack is especially relevant in regard to what we can label "equality rights," of which the right to welfare seems prominent. In the Marxian view, the use of the term "right" is incompatible with any sense of meaningful material equality. The attack on juridical language could not only be launched against all the theorists we have been examining in Part II, but against my entire project in this text. After all, I have proceeded since the Introduction on the assumption that by examining debates about justice and equality, the reader will be in a better position to understand two of the most pressing public issues facing our polities today. In the Marxian view, however, such a project could only serve to detract from real understanding. By allowing these issues to be framed in terms of justice, have we been engaged in an exercise in rhetoric rather than a search for philosophical understanding?

Before it is possible to answer this question, we must first understand why Marx and his followers reject juridical terms and believe that they are a source of oppression rather than liberation. In Marx's view, the notion of an "equal right" is nonsensical. Rights, by their definition, are rights of inequality, tools of oppression. In his famous criticism of non-Marxian socialist groups, "The Critique of the Gotha Programme," Marx explains why he himself never employs juridical language. He claims that it would be a "crime" to embrace the terms "equal right" or "fair distribution," because while these ideas "in a certain period had some meaning . . . [they] have now become obsolete verbal rubbish."[1] This quote seems to be a reference to what is often seen as Marx's theoretical approach: dialectical materialism. According to this view, Marx conceives of all philosophical and political discourse as "superstructure" which has nothing to do with the real foundations of society, namely economics, defined as labor relations. It is impossible, according to Marx, to address inequalities without examining the structure of our entire economic system. In short, without an analysis of current capitalism, our discussion is doomed to be ineffectual. If the Marxian is correct, battles over rights can never lead to any real egalitarian distribution of property. Rights talk, like any purely theoretical discourse, is interpreted as superstructure, too abstract to use in an examination of the real relations of society.

While the appeal to economic relations in order to reject rights talk is a common strategy of thinkers in the Marxist tradition, Marx himself offered an even more detailed attack on the language of rights. His critique is especially useful because he focuses on why the notion and use of rights preclude any form of egalitarian property distribution. If he is correct, the thinkers we have examined who make egalitarian welfare rights central–namely, Rawls and Rousseau–are making nonsensical claims.

In "On the Jewish Question," Marx argues that all appeals to rights only serve to guarantee the existing relations of a given society. A society that attempts to change property inequalities through the notion of rights is doomed to failure. This is due to the abstract notion of a right. Rights secure formal equality in the public sphere, while at the same time allowing for the existence of a private sphere where personal egoism ensures that there is not material equality. Although a promise of equality usually accompanies the discussion of rights, Marx argues that this promise serves only to mask the harsh realities of oppression.

Marx takes the right to property as paradigmatic of the dual role that rights play: it is used to make a claim to equality, while all the while ensuring inequality. Although it is couched in moral terms, "the right to property is . . . the right to enjoy one's fortune and to dispose of it as one will."[2] While this criticism could legitimately be aimed at theorists such as Locke who do not call for equality of property, it could just as easily be aimed at Rawls and Rousseau. Although they argue for egalitarian property relations, their reliance on rights would preclude any real reform.

Is Marx correct that the notion of an egalitarian and material right, like the right to welfare, is impossible to achieve? Have we been operating on a false assumption throughout Part II, namely that the vocabulary of rights and justice can in fact bring about egalitarian relations and a right to welfare if justice demands it? Some theorists who wish to answer in the affirmative might argue that by relying on a juridical vocabulary, we have ignored the actual power dynamics that must be overcome to enact such a right. By discussing rights solely in terms of justice, and in the previous section in terms of constitutional provisions, we have, they would argue, ignored the fact that such change can occur only with an active movement to change the power dynamics of fundamentally unequal societies.

I think, however, that these charges are misplaced. By asking what it is that justifies a society, we have been concerned to discover first whether welfare is in fact a right that should be central to a conception of justice and the legitimate state. Only after such a question has been answered in the affirmative (and we have seen arguments which claim it should not) are questions of strategy appropriate. If it turns out that the language of rights does not work well as political rhetoric, this does not mean that we are mistaken in using it to discover if there really is a fundamental right to welfare. A framework grounded in a legitimate philosophy must motivate any legitimate political strategy. Our inquiry has been limited to the former project, but I do not see how this fact precludes any form of political action, juridical or not.

The attack seems especially misplaced when it is aimed at the welfarist view we have developed through the work of Rousseau and Rawls. These theorists argue for a type of society which would necessitate radical restructuring in many parts of the world. These juridical theorists hardly apologize for the status quo.

Notes

1   Marx, "The Critique of the Gotha Programme," in R. Tucker (ed.), *The Marx-Engels Reader* (New York: Norton and Co., 1972), p. 530.
2   Marx, "On The Jewish Question," in *The Marx-Engels Reader*, p. 43.

23 Distributive Justice, Property and the Right to Welfare

Despite the Marxian objection that the concept of distributive justice itself is anti-egalitarian, we have seen throughout Part II that the spectrum of accounts of the just society is vast. It includes welfarist theories devoted to establishing egalitarian distributions of wealth and libertarian accounts that find re-distributive policies to be a violation of justice. This section of the book has been devoted to exploring these diverse views of justice and their impact on positions in the current debate over the role of welfare in society.

I began by establishing the link between distributive justice and the welfare controversy. I then proceeded to examine a libertarian account of justice, explaining how Locke's absolute property right is incompatible with a view of the state which gives welfare a central priority. Many scholars who believe Locke gives welfare a role in the state would contest my libertarian reading of Locke. In my view, however, Locke's insistence that the state enforce private property rights is inconsistent with a welfarist position.

In stark contrast to Locke, Rousseau offers a conception of justice which gives a central priority to welfare. Since justice is based in the social contract and the general will, all citizens on his account are entitled to guaranteed welfare subsistence. Rousseau does retain the notion that there is a right to private property. This concept, however, does not pre-exist the state and is itself a reflection of the general will, which reconciles private property and an egalitarian distribution of wealth.

While Rousseau is clearly a welfarist, he is vague about what specific distribution of wealth and property is most egalitarian. Here the more contemporary work of John Rawls is helpful. Rawls's notion of the veil of ignorance shares much with Rousseau's notion of the general will. However, Rawls is more explicit about what type of distribution of wealth is most egalitarian. Specifically, Rawls argues that the difference principle is more egalitarian than a strictly equal distribution of wealth because free and equal citizens would choose it over any other distribution from behind the veil of ignorance. Rawls's position is clearly welfarist.

After examining Rawls's view, I went on to present alternatives to his welfarist conception of justice. Michael Walzer, we saw, argues for a conception of welfare rights within certain "spheres of justice." Health care, for instance, would never be denied to any citizen, according to Walzer, regardless of their lack of effort in society. Walzer's concept is compatible with certain workfarist views. Individuals might be guaranteed the minimum essentials in life, but the state could encourage work in order to obtain luxuries, for instance.

Gutmann and Thompson present a view which is explicitly workfarist. As we saw, these theorists argue for a concept of fair workfare in which able citizens are expected to work, but only in return for fair wages. To what extent, however, do Gutmann/Thompson and Walzer develop concepts of distributive justice distinct from the libertarian and welfare views we have spent the bulk of Part II developing?

I have deliberately avoided developing a separate workfarist conception of the state because I believe that both welfarist and libertarian concepts have a role for work. Contemporary workfarist advocates, I believe, usually fall into one of those two camps when it comes to justifications of the state. Despite serving as alternatives to Rawls, the Walzerian view as well as Gutmann and Thompson's are compatible, I believe, with welfarist views of the state. This is true for two reasons. First, while both views leave room for the state to encourage work, neither is incompatible with the notion that the state should guarantee basic needs. While neither advocates a basic income to support those who refuse to work, they do support programs to ensure that health care needs and basic food and shelter needs are met. Second, Gutmann and Thompson's view, in particular, offers incentives for work that I believe would lead most people who can work to do so on their own accord. While this is an empirical prediction, if true, it would mean that in practice fair workfare could not justifiably be called punishment.

While these two progressive workfare views are compatible with welfarist conceptions of the state, there are also some views of workfare that are compatible with libertarian conceptions. I argued in Chapter 16, for instance, that Locke provides for a conception whereby the state would force certain individuals to work. This view, however, stemmed from a conception of the state's primary role as that of protector of private property. The state provided work, I suggested, in order to serve this purpose. Work, on this view, was best understood not as relief but as a way of protecting private property through punishment for poverty.

In summary, neither welfarist nor libertarian justifications of the state are incompatible with the idea that the state should encourage and, at times, demand work. The type of justification that one has for the state, however, will drastically impact the type of workfare policy to which one is led. For libertarians, such policies will be harsh and akin to punishment. For welfarists, such policies will not threaten the basic needs of individuals and will be akin to incentives for work that individuals would freely choose.

Throughout Part II, I have attempted to demonstrate that the current controversy over whether the state should provide welfare is at root a debate about distributive justice. Welfarists can find strong support for their views in the theories of Rousseau and Rawls. Likewise, libertarians can find strong foundations for their views in the libertarian writings of Locke and Nozick.

Conclusion

Throughout this text I have endeavoured to show why the concepts of justice and equality are relevant to two of the most contentious issues in contemporary politics. As I explored the death penalty and welfare controversies, I sought to uncover the assumptions inherent within the most popular arguments presented in these debates. These assumptions, I argued, connect to some of the most important theories of punishment and distributive justice in the history of political philosophy.

I began Part I by dismissing the feeling of vengeance as irrelevant in deciding whether the death penalty is just. I went on to distinguish revenge from the more acceptable position that some crimes deserve to be punished. I argued that both pro and anti-death penalty positions could be developed from this premise. Those positions which emphasized desert and moral guilt were best understood within the philosophy of retributivism and the related philosophical position of deontology. At the same time, those pro and anti-death penalty positions which emphasized deterrence and cost were best understood within the utilitarian tradition. Before it is possible to evaluate whether the death penalty is just, I argued, one must come to terms with what justifies punishment in the first place.

In Part II, I attempted to examine the basis of arguments that are made by welfarists and libertarians. I began by connecting the libertarian position to the Lockean view that the primary purpose of the state is to protect private property. Later, I argued that the welfarist position is best understood within the context of the philosophy of Rawls and Rousseau. For both, property is grounded in a notion of equal citizenship. As a result, both Rawls and Rousseau are led to support a strong right to welfare. Both libertarian and welfarist positions, I argued, have room for work. The role work plays in a society, however, differs greatly depending on whether one has a libertarian or welfarist view of the state.

While I have not sought to champion one argument in either of these controversies, I believe I have demonstrated that the history of political philosophy, with its emphasis on justice and rights, is not mere ideology. I have shown that the history of ideas about justice provides a basis for those who disagree about the death penalty and welfare to examine their assumptions and engage in real argument. It is my hope that this text will be of use to people interested in examining the foundations of these discussions. I hope to have offered a springboard for those who would like to join in an ancient conversation about justice, a conversation which I have argued is still relevant to our contemporary political debates.

Bibliography

Baird, R.M. and Rosenbaum, S.E. (eds) (1995) *Punishment and the Death Penalty* (Amherst, NY: Prometheus Books).

Berlin, I. (1990) *Four Essays On Liberty* (Oxford: Oxford University Press).

Brettschneider, C.L. (1998) "From Liberalism to the End of Juridical Language: An Examination of the Early Marx's Jurisprudence," in A. Sarat and P. Ewick (eds), *Studies in Law, Politics, and Society*, Volume 18 (Greenwich, CT: JAI Press).

Dworkin, R. (1986) *Law's Empire* (Cambridge, MA: Harvard University Press).

Feinberg, J. (ed.) (1995) *Philosophy of Law* (Belmont: Wadsworth).

Feinberg, J. (ed.) (1993) *Reason and Responsibility* (Belmont: Wadsworth).

Gutmann, A. and Thompson, D. (1996) *Democracy and Disagreement* (Cambridge, MA: Belknap Press of Harvard University Press).

Holmes, S. (1995) *Passions and Constraints: On the Theory of Liberal Democracy* (Chicago: University of Chicago Press).

Kant, I. (1965) *The Metaphysical Elements of Justice* (New York: Macmillan).

Kant, I. (1959) *Foundations of the Metaphysics of Morals* (New York: Macmillan).

Kateb, G. (1994) *The Inner Ocean* (New York: Cornell University Press).

Kripke, S.A. (1982) *Wittgenstein on Rules and Private Language* (Cambridge, MA: Harvard University Press).

Lewis, C.S. (1993) "The Humanitarian Theory of Punishment," in Feinberg, J. (ed.) *Reason and Responsibility* (Belmont: Wadsworth).

Locke, J. (1993) *Political Writings* (ed. and introduction D. Wootton) (London and New York: Penguin Books).

Marx, K. (1972) "The Critique of the Gotha Programme," in R. Tucker (ed.) *The Marx-Engels Reader* (New York: Norton and Co.).

Marx, K. (1972) "On the Jewish Question," in R. Tucker (ed.) *The Marx-Engels Reader* (New York: Norton and Co.).

Mill, J.S. and Bentham, J. (1997) *Utilitarianism and Other Essays* (ed. A. Ryan) (London: Penguin Books).

Nietzsche, F. (1989) *On the Genealogy of Morals* (trans. N. Kaufman) (New York: Vintage Books).

Nagel, R. (1981) *Philosophical Explanations* (Cambridge, MA: Harvard University Press.

Nozick, R. (1974) *Anarchy, State, Utopia* (New York: Basic Books).

Parijis, P. van (1991) "Why Surfers Should Be Fed: The Liberal Case For An Unconditional Basic Income," *Philosophy and Public Affairs*, 20 (Spring).

Rachels, J. (1986) *The Elements of Moral Philosophy* (Philadelphia: Temple University Press).

Rawls, J. (1996) *Political Liberalism* (New York: Columbia University Press).

Rawls, J. (1995) "Two Concepts of Rules," in J. Feinberg (ed.), *Philosophy of Law* (Belmont: Wadsworth).

Rawls, J. (1971) *A Theory of Justice* (Cambridge, MA: Belknap Press of Harvard University Press).

Reich, C. (1990) "Beyond the New Property: An Ecological View of Due Process," *Brooklyn Law Review*, 56 (Summer).

Reich, C. (1964) "The New Property," *Yale Law Journal*, 73.

Rorty, R. (1989) *Contingency, Irony and Solidarity* (Cambridge: Cambridge University Press).

Rousseau, J.J. (1987) *The Basic Political Writings* (Indianapolis, IN: Hackett).

Sarat, A. (1999) *The Killing State: Capital Punishment in Law, Politics and Culture* (Oxford: Oxford University Press).

Thompson, J. (1971) "A Defense of Abortion," *Philosophy and Public Affairs*, 1 (Fall).

Van den Haag, E. and Conrad, J.P. (1983) *The Death Penalty: A Debate* (New York: Plenum Publishing), reprinted in *The Death Penalty: Opposing Viewpoints* (1997).

Walzer, M. (1983) *Spheres of Justice: A Defense of Pluralism and Equality* (New York: Basic Books).

Weil, G.L. (1973) *The Long Shot: George McGovern Runs for President* (New York: Norton).

Williams, B. (1971) *Morality: An Introduction to Ethics* (New York: Harper Collins, 1971).

Winter, P. (ed.) (1997) *The Death Penalty* (San Diego, CA: Greenhaven).

Index

abuse, criminals as victims of 40–41
abuse of justice 45, 102
acceptance of inequality 10–14, 123
"adequate standards provision" 136–7
Aid to Families with Dependent
    Children 77
amour propre 101
anger 43–4
anti-foundationalism 8
apartheid 4
appeals against conviction 36
attention-seeking criminals 23
autonomy of individuals 113, 127

behavioural psychology 28–9
Bentham, Jeremy 51–2, 54–5
Berlin, Isaiah 84, 106
Blackman, Justice 16–18
Brennan, Justice 60–70 *passim*
Brown vs. *Board of Education* 45

Callins vs. *Collins* 16–17
capital punishment
    constitutionality of *see* United
        States Constitution: and capital
        punishment
    discriminatory application of 7, 19,
        69
    effectiveness at a given time 68
    relevance of any social benefits of
        60–61
    seen as degrading to human dignity
        66–7, 70
    usual form of debates about 2–3, 5,
        8–9, 13, 147–8

variable enforcement of 68–70
    see also execution
"categorical imperative" 59, 61
charity 87, 90–94
child labour 92
coercion
    freedom from 106–7
    into work 91–3
collective interests of society 103–5
compatibilism and incompatibilism 38
conscience 44–5
consensus on principles of justice 116
consequences, relevance of 48; *see*
        also utilitarianism
constitutional rights
    of slaves 45
    to welfare 78–9, 81, 135–6
    see also United States Constitution:
        and capital punishment
cruelty
    of criminals 17
    of the death penalty 16, 36, 63, 65–8

Dead Man Walking (film) 16
death penalty *see* capital punishment
death row 15–16, 36, 66
decision-making, political 48
democratic government 105–6
deontology 49, 58–60, 147
dependency on government programs
        77
desert, concept of
    applied to capital punishment 30–31,
        33, 35–7, 49, 54, 60–61, 67, 70
    applied to welfare 80, 147

determinism 38–40
deterrence 13, 23–5, 30–31, 33, 40, 43, 45, 47–8, 52–3, 68–9, 147
  singular as distinct from general 27–8, 31
dialectical materialism 140
difference principle 118–24, 125, 136, 143
  determination of compliance with 122
disabled people, welfare provision for 93
"distinctness of persons" 134
distribution of wealth 2–3, 7, 9, 73–4, 100–104, 123, 144
  irrespective of desert 119
  just and unjust 104–5
  see also redistribution
distributive justice 3, 9, 73–4, 80, 117, 126, 143–5
  legitimate and illegitimate systems of 100–103
  Locke's position on 87–8, 94
  Marxist critique of whole concept 81–2, 139–41
  Rousseau's position on 97–8
  welfare provision needed for 108
Douglas, Justice 69–70
duelling 61

effort, rewards for 85, 115, 129–30
egalitarian principles and procedures 7, 81, 108, 116, 140–41, 143
Eighth Amendment to the US Constitution (on "cruel and unusual punishment") 65–8
electrocution 16, 36
emotional reactions 16–19
  as a basis for punishment 19, 21–2
empathy 15–17
Enlightenment thought 8
equality 7, 69, 147
  of interests 111, 113
  of opportunity 118
  see also inequality

"equality rights" 139–40
ethical theories 48–9
execution
  delays prior to 36
  demonstrations associated with 15
  methods of 16–17, 62–3
"eye for an eye" philosophy see lex talionis

fairness, justice as 112–13
Feinberg, J. 66
flogging 66
foundationalism 8
Fourteenth Amendment to the US Constitution (on equal application of the law) 69
"free and equal citizens" 111
free-rider problem 81, 129–32
free will 38–40
freedom, negative 84
Furman vs. Georgia 65–71

gas chambers 16, 36
"general will" of society 97, 103, 107–8, 111, 143
genetics 28–9
good life, the, individual concepts of 116, 118, 120, 127
government
  absence of 19
  see also state, the
Gregg vs. Georgia 65, 68, 70
guilt
  feelings of 44
  as a necessary condition for punishment 53, 57, 59–61
Gutmann, Amy and Thompson, Dennis Democracy and Disagreement 80–81, 130–31, 144

hard work, rewards of 85, 115, 129–30
health care 126–7, 144
Hobbes, Thomas 104
Holmes, Stephen 89–91
human dignity, denial of 63, 66–7, 70

humanitarian theories 30–31

ideology, arguments from 3–6, 147
illegitimate children, mothers' murder
  of 61
individuals
  promotion of well-being of 103–4
  respect for 54, 59
  see also autonomy; good life;
    liberty; rights
inequality
  acceptance of 101–4, 123
  in access to "primary goods" 118–19
  in distribution of property generally
    85, 87; *see also* distribution of
    wealth
  justifications for 111, 119
  legitimization of 100
inheritance 85
insanity of defendants 38
intelligence, moral arbitrariness of 85,
  115

Jackson vs. *Bishop* 66
"just punishment" 30–31, 48, 51
"just society," the 8–9, 99, 112, 119,
  136, 143
"just state," the 7–8, 119, 127

Kant, Immanuel 49, 59–61, 63
  The Metaphysical Elements of Justice
    61
King, Martin Luther 34

labour
  of children 92
  forced 91–3
  ownership of the products of 84,
    100–101
  see also refusal to work; right to
    work; work incentives
language 98–9
  of justice 4–5, 139–41
legitimacy for a society or state 7–8,
  87

lethal injection 16, 36, 66
Lewis, C.S.: *God in the Dock* 30–31
lex talionis 13, 15, 18, 34
libertarian thought 78–83, 87–90, 94,
  122–3, 133–6, 143–7
liberty
  distribution of 121, 122–3
  individual 105–6
  infringements of 123
  positive and negative concepts of
    106–7
  protection of 127
  rights to 117–18, 122
  value of 136
  variations in worth of 124
life imprisonment 27, 35, 67
Locke, John 7–9, 19, 21, 34, 80–94,
  97–108, 112, 114, 119, 123, 135,
  139–40, 143–7
  "Draft of a Representation containing
    a Scheme of Methods for the
    Employment of the Poor" 91
  First Treatise on Government 90
  Second Treatise on Government 18,
    89–90
luck 85
luxuries, subsidization of 126

McGovern, George 77–8
"Malibu surfer" problem 130–31
Marx, Karl
  "Critique of the Gotha Programme"
    140
  "On the Jewish Question" 140
  theory of 3–4, 6, 73–4, 81–2, 139–41
maximin strategy 117–24 *passim*, 125,
  136–7
means to an end 59–60, 70
Medicaid 127
mens rea, principle of 38
meritocratic views of justice 115
minimum income guarantees 77–8,
  125
minors, punishment of 35
mitigating circumstances 41, 61–2

mnemotechnics 44
money, use of 89, 91
moral obligations 87, 90
moral relativism 5–6, 37
moral rights 79, 90–91, 94
morality
  basis for 37
  flouting of 39
  theories of 33–4
  "universal law" of 59–60, 62
motivations of criminals 61–2

natural justice 106
natural law and natural rights 7–8,
    83–7, 97–8, 101–3
naturally-justified traits 114–15
needs as a justification for welfare
    rights 81, 120–22, 126–7
New York City criminal court 3
The New York Times 78
Nietzsche, Frederick 6, 14, 22, 40,
    43–5, 61, 73, 81
Nixon, Richard 78
"noble savage," the 98–9
Nozick, Robert 7, 9, 38–9, 41, 80–81,
    112, 133–4, 135, 139, 145
  Anarchy, State and Utopia 133
Nygaard, Richard 31

objections to justice 3–7
obligations to society 41, 131–2
"original position," the 111–15, 123

pain
  avoidance of 51–2
  infliction of 36, 66–7
"perfectionist theories" 120
philosophical foundations for popularly-
    held positions 8; *see also*
    political philosophy
pity 17–18, 33
Plato 1, 7–8
pleasure, pursuit of 51–3
political action, scope for 141
political philosophy 48, 80, 147–8

post-modernism 8
poverty
  and the concept of justice 100, 102
  and crime 40–41
  maintained in the general interest
    104
  reasons for existence of 91
power 4–5, 73
  property as an assertion of 100–102
  sense of responsibility as a by-
    product of 44–5
  states as instruments of 139, 141
practicality of solutions to philosophical
    questions 22
pragmatism 39–40
prediction of criminal activity 28
prejudice 7, 19, 69
"priests," vengeful motives of 43–4
primary goods 117–24 *passim*, 125–7,
    136
  inequalities in 118–19
principles of justice
  choice of 113–16
  and distribution of welfare 121
propensity to commit crime 29
property ownership 80, 83–5, 102,
    106, 136, 140, 143
  inequalities in worth of 124
  Locke's position on 103–4
  Rawls position on 123–4
  Rousseau's position on 97–107
  state protection for 83, 86–7, 90,
    93–4, 102, 106
  and wastage or spoilage of property
    88–9, 91
punishment
  based on emotional reactions 21–2
  based on vengeance 18–22
  capricious 54, 69–70
  consensus with regard to 37
  consistency and inconsistency in
    18–25 *passim*, 29, 53–4
  criminals excused from 53
  degrees of seriousness in 35
  effect on society at large 51

effectiveness of 68, 71
excessive 25, 28–37 *passim*, 53, 55, 58, 66–7
fitting the crime 33
humanitarian theory of 30–31
hybrid theories of 14, 57–8
of innocent people 24, 28, 33, 53–8, 104
irrelevant influences on 53
just and unjust conceptions of 45–8; *see also* just punishment
state's organization of 43
usual form of debates about 2–3
work as a form of 93–4

rape 35
rationality 106–7
Rawls, John 7–9, 41, 57–8, 80–81, 105, 108, 111–47 *passim*
Political Liberalism 136
Reagan, Ronald 77
reciprocity, principle of 81, 132–4
redistribution 80–81, 87, 105–6, 116, 119, 123, 125, 135, 137
of the fruits of people's talents and labour 134
"reflective equilibrium" 8
refusal to work 92, 130–31
rehabilitation of offenders 27, 29–31, 38, 40
Reich, Charles: "The New Property" 78
relativism *see* moral relativism
relevance of debates about justice 1–3
responsibility
as a by-product of power 44–5
of the criminal 38–41
retribution as distinct from revenge 31, 33–4
retributive punishment, formula for 38–9, 41
retributivism 3, 9, 13–14, 35–6, 43–9, 52, 57–60, 65–70, 73, 147
objections to 6, 61–2
revenge as a justification for punishment 13–22, 31–4, 43, 61, 147

rhetoric of justice 101–2, 141, 143
right to have rights 67
right to work 88
rightness, principle of 51
rights
distribution of 117
enforcement of 124
"formal" and "material" 135–6
"inalienable" 86
individual 54, 112
moral as distinct from political 79, 90–91, 94
negative 90–91
see also constitutional rights; "equality rights"; liberty; natural law; property ownership; welfare rights
risk aversion 117, 132
Rousseau, Jean-Jacques 7–8, 80–83, 94, 97–106, 111–12, 115, 139–47 *passim*
Discourse on Inequality 98
Discourse on Political Economy 104
rule utilitarianism 55, 57
rules, breaking of 55

Scalia, Justice 17–18
segregation, racial 45
self-ownership 83–4
slavery 4, 45, 73–4, 86
social construction
of justice 108
of rights 124
social contract 81, 86, 101–3, 144
social goods 120, 125
social meaning of goods 125–6
social utility 54–5, 57, 68
social welfare policy 111
socialization 116
society at large
effect of punishment on 51
collective interests of 103–5
instability in 62
obligations to 41, 131–2
overall well-being of 24

responsibility of 40
see also "just society"
South Africa 79
starving to death 93–4
state, the
  obligations of 126, 130
  responsibility for protection of
    property 83, 86–7, 90, 93–4,
    102, 106
  role of 78–81, 86–7, 105, 108, 123,
    139, 147
  theory of 8
  see also "just state"
"state of nature" 19, 34, 84, 97–9
suicide 86
Supreme Court *see* United States
    Constitution: and capital
    punishment

talent, value of 85, 115, 129–30, 133
  conferred by society 134
taxation 87, 105, 108
theories of justice 7, 81
Thompson, Dennis *see* Gutmann,
    Amy
trivialization of offences 35

United States
  health care in 127
  hostility towards notion of welfare in
    105
United States Constitution
  and capital punishment 16–17, 36,
    47–8, 65–71
  Eighth Amendment 65–8
  Fourteenth Amendment 69
  libertarian guarantees in 135
  and slavery 45
  welfare rights embedded in 78–9

utilitarianism 9, 48, 51–60, 65, 68–9,
    147
  "rule" and "act" types of 55
utils 51, 54

van den Haag, E. 34–5, 70
"veil of ignorance" 81, 112–33 *passim*,
    143
vengeance *see* revenge
vulgar relativism 5

Walzer, Michael 80–81, 127–9
  Spheres of Justice 125, 144
wealth
  aggregate amount of 118
  see also distribution of wealth;
    redistribution
welfare rights 80–81, 103, 107–8,
    122–3, 139–43
  baseline level for 119–20, 144
  for children 79
  guarantees of 136–7, 144
  Locke's position on 83, 90, 94, 97
  meaning of 79
  in the United States 77–8
  unrelated to needs 120–21
  usual form of debates about 2–5, 8–9,
    147–8
"welfarism" 78–81
White, Justice 65, 68–71
Williams, Bernard 5–6
Wisconsin model of welfare provision
    77
Wittgenstein, Ludwig 39
work incentives 130, 144–5
workfare 78–81, 88, 130, 144–5

zero-sum game 118